Cheese Market of the Future

& other stories

A collection of short stories by

Dewi Heald

First published by Dream Jellyhouse in print
on demand in 2016

Copyright ©Dewi Heald 2016

Photography Copyright © Dewi Heald 2016

Front cover generously manipulated
by Steve Scaddan

The right of Dewi Heald to be identified as
the Author of the Work has been asserted by
him in accordance with the Copyright,
Designs and Patents Act 1988.

Dedication

This book is dedicated to all the wrong people.

A Word on Design

It has been said that oriental rugs have one error woven into them as only God is perfect. This book uses this same principle. If you find the error, then the mistake is mine. If you find the error and then keep looking for others, then the mistake is yours.

CONTENTS

Cheese Market of the Future

"What do you think?" asked the Professor as he removed his wife's blindfold.

"You've tidied the attic!" she exclaimed in wonderment.

The Professor sighed heavily and pointed across the attic to the wardrobe propped up against the beams of the roof.

"The wardrobe?" pondered Linda, "Have you put all your clothes up here, John?"

John sighed again. He had sighed a lot during his marriage to Linda, especially since he retired and devoted his days to creating inventions in the attic. Before he married Linda he would have called it a loft. She would call it a potential fourth bedroom to add value to the house. There were many gaps between them, only one of which was age. His frustration now was caused by the fact that he had finally invented something worth seeing. He was not a real Professor (as his wife had once reminded him during a bitter and never-talked-about argument) but, by goodness, he had actually managed to create something incredible, something that should truly cause wonder. He wondered why Linda could not see it.

Linda smiled politely. She had spent a long time smiling politely during her marriage to John.

"This, my darling," he enthused, "is not just a wardrobe. Yes, I have chosen the design deliberately. Perhaps C.S.Lewis's estate will sue should I ever sell it, but ... ah, no, I have created something incredible. In this wardrobe is the secret to time travel."

Linda was not sure what to say. In the three years since her husband retired, she had seen automated pan-scrubbers, kite-flyers and gardening kits come down from the attic, but nothing quite like what he was describing now. She cautiously moved across the crawling boards and tip-toed over to the invention. Even in her attic, she wore high-heeled shoes. She glanced back towards John for a little re-assurance and, when he nodded excitedly, she tentatively opened one of the doors. Her eyes immediately lighted on a mass of incredible colours, swirling in odd directions and patterns before her eyes.

"Well, what can I say?" she said when she had caught her breath, "I never thought you were going to put those awful Hawaiian shirts away. I told you that you were too old now, dear."

"Behind the shirts!" snapped the Professor. His feet were louder and more determined than hers on the crawling boards and he grabbed the wardrobe door in one hand and pushed the shirts aside with the other. "If I walk through the back of this wardrobe, I will be transported into the future. I have chosen a wardrobe because I believe that these items of furniture will always exist. I can cleverly locate another wardrobe and use it to make my return. This is revolutionary. This is incredible. This should strike you dumb with wonder, damn it!"

6

"It's very nice, dear," replied Linda as she turned and walked back towards the door, "Dinner's almost ready. I'll serve, if you can open a bottle of wine for me."

The Professor looked on with familiar exasperation. A dull academic marriage had ended in divorce fifteen years earlier and Linda, his smart and well-dressed secretary had been the one to listen to him and bring him out of his self-defeat. However, she had never really appreciated his inventions or encouraged him. Maybe she needed to see the proof in front of her to understand just how this miracle of physics had occurred in the loftspace - not atticspace - of her house.

"I'll travel into the future after dinner, then!" he called after her. This was not exactly how H.G.Wells had said it would be.

* * * * *

Time Travel Diary, Entry One –

Thursday, March 1st (St David's Day) 2012

This is the first entry in my time travel diary. I, Professor John Harding Ellis, have decided to record my first forays into the future. It is evening (after dinner) and I am in the loft of 14, Tremorfa Terrace, Cardiff. I will explain the design later, for now I will make the historic step into a future we can only dream of ...

... I am now in the future and this has to be more of an unusual experience than anyone could predict. I emerged in a wardrobe at the back of some kind of storage room – the walls were white and the room full of boxes. I made tentative steps out of the room and found myself, to my astonishment, in a Market. The people eyed me suspiciously and I did not talk too much in case language had changed in this year. The room led on to a cheese stall and I was amazed by the range of cheese available. Clearly society has broken down in the future and supermarkets cannot exist to sell these items. I counted thirty or forty on this one stall alone and noted others – all shapes, all names on several others nearby. The agricultural economy must have grown more healthy to cope with local demand following the collapse of the supermarket system. Not wanting to create too much disturbance, I bought some cheese from the stall-owner (some odd-looking Y Fenni) and ran back to the wardrobe. My currency was accepted – some co-ordination of our current world must therefore exist ...

* * * * *

"Mustard ... yes, that's it, mustard," said Linda Ellis as she served her new dish.

"Now, why would it contain mustard?" asked her husband, "I wonder what it means."

"Well, dear, you can get mustard in cheese at the moment. I'll have a look for it at the shops if you like. Don't forget we've got Lucy and Nick coming round tomorrow – it would be nice to surprise them with something unusual. Could you get something else at the Cheese Market of the Future?"

The Professor kissed his wife on the lips and smiled. Finally, she seemed to understand.

*   *   *   *   *

Time Travel Diary, Entries Two to Five

March 12th – March 22nd 2012

I have made three more trips since I last wrote. I will admit that the excitement of Linda's support in this enterprise has made me slightly more daring. I have managed to purchase a large amount of future cheese (at reasonable prices – why so little inflation?) and we certainly shocked Lucy and Nick who were quite amazed by some of the Llangloffan I had bought – checked map, it's the name of a small village in Pembrokeshire. I am certain that this is further indication of the demise of city life in future time.

Let me tell you briefly about the trips – each one has become more risky as the stall-owner is becoming more suspicious of me emerging from his storeroom. Even buying cheese from him does not placate him. His rising anger suggests that my interpretation of society having fragmented or broken down is correct.

I have explored the market further. It is clearly Victorian in construction (how many others of these buildings have survived?) and has a high vaulted ceiling. The stalls are crammed into rows and almost all seem to stock cheese. I am hoping on future journeys to leave the market and explore the world outside. What kind of scene of desolation awaits me there ...?

* * * * *

"John, honey ..." said Linda as she stood by the cooker, stirring the cheese sauce slowly. She spoke deliberately and carefully, her words well-rehearsed.

"What is it?" asked her husband, looking up from his notes on a journey that had brought him some new ideas and a block of Caws Celtica. Frankly, it was over-priced for 2012, let alone the future.

Linda dried her hands and smoothed down her purple dress. It was the dress she wore when she wanted something. It was the kind of garment that clung to her in a way that would suggest to her husband that he knew what she wanted ... and while he was distracted by thinking about that, she could get what she really wanted from him.

"John, dear," she started again, "It's been three months now since you started buying cheese and, well ... I don't know quite how to put this to you ... but, well, it's just that cheese is getting a bit ... old."

"You mean it's going off?"

"Not really, it's just that all our friends have tasted it now." she said as she sat down at the table next to him and smoothed his arm. "It's not that I don't appreciate how wonderful this invention has been – we would never have been able to entertain our friends so well without it, but I just think that we have done all we can with it."

"I know you must be disappointed that I have not ventured further. Maybe I have been afraid. Maybe so – we are looked at a world that has retreated to an agricultural economy, a world where a man shouts at me just because I pick up cheese from his stall and retreat into the storeroom. I don't want to push scientific discovery too far."

She tried stroking his arm a little more as she replied softly, "That's lovely dear, it truly is. Yes, if you were going to go on to a smoked sausage stall or something then I would understand. But you have to understand that I miss you. You are never here in the evenings and you sit there writing up your observations during the day. I thought when you retired that we would spend more time together, not less. John, darling, how about calling it a day?"

The Professor sighed and moved his wife's arm back on to the table. He spoke – "Linda. I have been inventing for three years now. I cannot even begin to explain how I came across something so fantastic as this. While you've been working, I have been working too. I don't even quite understand how this invention works, a lot of it was guesswork – if I lost my wardrobe now I don't even think I could build it again. But it could change humanity, we could see the effects of our actions!"

"Can't you see the effect your actions are having on me?" she replied, with a flick of her brown hair and a clenched fist tapping the table impatiently.

"I know you're disappointed with me. I will make up for it," he pushed his glasses up his nose, "tonight I will leave the market and go out in to the world. I was hoping to purchase a small pistol for my own protection before doing this, but I take that risk for you."

The Professor rose and marched upstairs, his feet heavy on the stairs.

"But your dinner!" his wife yelled after him as he started his mission.

*   *   *   *   *

The Professor's last journey was, even by his own low standards, a disappointment. Emerging from the wardrobe, he found the stall-holder waiting for him. The communication with the future-being, possibly mankind's first attempt to talk to its future self, was an apology and an assurance that he was not hoarding cheese in an abandoned wardrobe nor had he just escaped from Whitchurch mental hospital as the stall-holder seemed to think. The communication ended with the Professor running, the sound of a cheese-seller smashing up an old wardrobe ringing ominously in his ears. How would he ever return?

When would he see Linda again? Would someone steal his invention? He knew he could not recreate it for sure and, if it fell into the wrong hands ...

The Professor ran more out of panic than anything. He had no idea which way to run but he snaked between different stalls, his heart pounding in his chest and his breath short and weak. All these people looking so normal and yet looking at him strangely. Had the cheese-seller gone? He wheezed to a halt by a phone booth. He rubbed the sweat from his forehead with a handkerchief and drew what breath he had left. He would now have no choice but to try to live among these people. He waved away one of them who asked if he was alright – that made him smile, these people could be his friends after all. Maybe he could prove that he was from the past and make a small fortune from that?

Back in an attic in Cardiff, Linda was wearing her best party clothes. She had taken good care of herself over the years – she thought that having no children had helped to preserve the curves of her figure - and she had never lost her love of applying the right make-up and clothes to fight the onset of the future. The clothes had hung for too long at the back of her wardrobe while clothes designed for entertaining at home had hung at the front. Now she was determined to recreate a bit of behaviour from the past.

Linda still had friends – the ones who moaned that she never went out anymore – and, more to the point, she was still on good terms with the lads who had worked on refurbishing the University buildings when she worked there. Those were the same men that were now smashing up the old wardrobe in the attic and were about to take her up on her offer of joining her and her friends on a night out. They had turned down an offer of dinner – they said it 'smelt a bit cheesy'.

The Professor took a deep breath. He had spent more than a few minutes regaining his breath. He was not as fit as he was in the past. He might try exercising in future. But for now, he fixed his eyes on the large stained-glass doors that had Spring sunlight flowing through them. Another deep breath for luck and he prized one of the doors open.

He could see hills and little terraced houses. It was unmistakably a South Wales scene. Was this what Cardiff had come to – a rural cheese centre? There was some quiet and he noted the signs of technological progress – a fair number of satellite dishes, a few cars from his day parked up on the pavement; maybe that was even a wind farm on a hill in the distance. The Professor smiled as he had always had a soft spot for environmentally-friendly technology and this seemed to satisfy him that the world would not go completely mad. Then he crossed the empty road and looked behind him.

Linda locked the door and smiled to herself. She had dressed with a little more daring than before. Her mobile phone rang and she waved to the car across the street. Sarah would wait while she tried to find that damned phone.

* * * * *

The Professor stepped in to the machine that would move him through time and space. This one could take more than one passenger but you had to pay for the journey. No-one else in the machine looked particularly happy. This journey would move him back to Cardiff for sure – the whole process would take an hour. He set the alarm on his watch in case he fell asleep.

He sat down on an empty seat and sighed heavily as the bus pulled away from the stop on its way to Cardiff. He looked back wryly at the sign on the outside of the market – "The Abergavenny Cheese Festival 2012".

Advice for Advice-Givers

In past writings, I have alluded to the story of how Naomi Wolf gave up writing for a while after being offered vagina-shaped pasta at a party. This story was written following a similar pause in my writing, though I do not quite think that the cause was the same (I will save my writers-block-caused-by-pasta-shaped-as-genitalia for another time).

This was written during a particularly traumatic time in my life. My marriage had broken down and I was left trying to redecorate and sell a large home as well as my life having been turned upside down. I needed support and help, but I realised that most people wanted to offer me something else – advice.

Advice is the junk mail of conversation. No-one really wants it, it rarely receives attention and yet it still just keeps on coming. People give advice (it is always given and never offered, truly it is the gift you never wanted) and they mistake it for help. Let me put it like this – if you are stuck at the bottom of a deep hole, help is throwing down a rope, advice is shouting 'you should never have fallen down a hole'.

It seemed as though everybody wanted to give me advice. This is not quite true, all you lovely people reading this will not be those kind of people, but there are a lot of other people who really wanted to give me advice. Barclays Bank even offered me advice - they advised me to take out a £25k loan at competitive rates. That was probably some of the least predictable advice too.

I noticed this tendency last year and longed to have the rudeness to interrupt the advice-giver and tell him where to stick her or his advice. Recently a good friend wrote to me and used the wonderful words, "I can't give you any advice, but I am willing to listen." Oh if only the advice-givers of the world could understand that their number is huge but the number of listeners is small! Over the months since, I have been collecting some of the following gems and what I would really like to say to them. Welcome to my festival of rudeness!

By the way, as things stand, you can offer me pasta in any shape you like.

NOW READ ON

- If you want my advice ...

- Hold on, let me just think ... well ... hmm ... you know what, turns out I **don't** want your advice.

- In my experience ...

- And in my experience, your experience is tedious and worthless.

- You know what your problem is?

- Is it people trying to tell me what my problem is?

- If you ask me ...

- Well, that's why I didn't.

- You know what you should do ...

- Ignore everything else in that sentence?

- If I were you ..

- If you were me you'd worry about why cheese goes mouldy and whether you have too many purple shirts so you probably haven't got the concept yet.

- You know what I think?

- You think that for some strange reason I care what you think?

- I can't imagine what that must be like for you.

- Good. Talk to me when you can.

And the one that started this all was ...

- Do you want my advice?

- No, not particularly.

(As a technical note, my school's PE teacher-turned-careers-advisor, Mr Stoneham once said to me, 'Do you know what your problem is, Heald?'. I had not yet come up with the reply above so, instead, I went for the false innocence of, "No, I don't ... what is my problem?". Clearly thinking that he was saying something outstandingly profound, he said, "Your problem is that you are too laid-back." Well, how could I resist the obvious joke? I looked like I was thinking about it, pondering it, chewing it over, considering the wise words that he had said and then after a little while replied, "Oh well, can't be helped. What else?").

Denial is the Best Moisturiser

Today sees the launch of 'Denial', a new moisturiser that we believe will take the UK by storm. Denial is aspirational, controversial and the ultimate complementary product for a young woman's skin care regime. Let us have a look at the first advert, due to appear on YouTube and social media later today.

Jenny and Penny are young women who share a flat in a nondescript urban area. They are preparing for a night out. Jenny is horrified to see that Penny is not yet getting ready.

"Penny! What are you doing? It's nearly eight and you haven't started on your skin care regime?"

"Oh that," replies Penny with nonchalance, "I've said goodbye to all that now I have Denial."

"Denial?"

"Yes, Denial, it's the new moisturiser that takes years off your looks and gives hours back to your life."

Penny hands Jenny a small tub, which Jenny opens and eyes suspiciously. Penny points to the labelling.

"Look, it's scientifically formulated and is rose-tinted to make your future even better," she says.

"But Penny, this tub looks like it's empty to me. Does this stuff actually work?"

"Look at my skin - don't you think that I look younger, my skin is firmer and ... well, I would say that I am challenging the signs of ageing but since I've had Denial, I don't think I am ageing!"

"You're right - you do look better!"

"That's thanks to Denial."

"Maybe I should try it - Denial ..."

"Hey! Get your own!"

They both laugh and the caption appears - "Denial : Let Your Misplaced Confidence Shine Through."

*   *   *   *   *

The National Cosmetics Association has complained today about Denial, a new brand of moisturiser that has been taking the nation by storm since it was launched. The NCA is drawing attention to the untested nature of Denial and questions about its ingredients. A spokeswoman for the trade association said -

"We are very concerned about Denial. The beauty industry spends millions of pounds each year thoroughly researching and testing ways to make women feel unattractive and that our products are the only solution. There is no evidence that Denial has been tested in any such way. Furthermore, the manufacturers are talking about ingredients such as 'inner confidence' and 'feeling happy about yourself' that have never had their chemical composition tested. We are demanding that Denial is withdrawn from sale immediately so that women can return to fighting the signs of ageing by buying our products."

* * * * *

The Davina Heald Foundation, makers of the best-selling Denial has released a new advert that seeks to take on some of the fears of its critics and which aims at a new audience. Here it is -

TV and radio personality Richard Bacon is sitting on a busy commuter train, somewhere near Cadoxton. There are two women sitting next to him at the train table. He speaks -

"Hi, I'm Richard Bacon and I'm here to find out what real women think of Denial."

He turns to the woman on his right.

"Tell me Sandra, you're a real woman. You've been combating the signs of ageing using Denial. How have you found it?"

"It's been great, Kevin. Since swapping over to Denial, I have never felt better."

"And on the happiness scale - where would you rate yourself now?"

"I've never felt better, Kevin."

Bacon moves further down the carriage and sits next to another young woman. He speaks -

"Sandra's friend Barbara has another opinion, don't you, Barbara?"

"Yes, Kevin. I just don't see the advantages of Denial. I think that you should see your problems and then worry about them. That's always been the way for women, I don't think that Denial will help."

"And tell me Barbara, tell me about the other women in this train carriage?"

"Well, the woman over there has much better hair than me ... and there's that woman who always does really good eye shadow and ..."

Bacon stands and walks down the train carriage towards the camera.

"In an international scientifically-proven study, an astonishing 92% of all women who use Denial alone to fight the signs of ageing report feelings of happiness and well-being."

The carriage occupants turn to the camera and say in unison, "Denial : Let your misplaced confidence shine through."

* * * * *

Following on from the rapid success of both Denial and the up-market 'Avoidance' brand, the manufacturer of these products is expanding its range with 'Denial : Pour Homme'. The latest advert follows -

Gary is sitting in the front room in front of a large flat screen television. There are bowls of crisps and cans of beer surrounding him. Barry enters the room, having just been upstairs. He is carrying a small grey-coloured tube, which he throws towards Gary.

"Oy mate! Since when have you wanted to smell like a woman?"

"This? This is 'Denial : Pour Homme', it's for men."

"Rubbish."

"Look - it says so here, 'specially formulated for men' and the tube is all grey and dynamic-looking. Not a trace of pink in sight, it's for men, see."

"What does it do then?"

"It keeps my skin moisturised."

"'Cos you can never be too careful with dry skin?"

"You'd be surprised."

"Yeah, but if I start using products on my skin ... won't that mean I'm gay?"

"No," replied Gary with outrage, "using skin care products does not mean you are gay. It's having sex with your boyfriend that does that."

"Oh yeah, I'd forgotten that."

The screen caption reads : "Denial. Just Do It."

*   *   *   *   *

The beauty world has been rocked by the news that the Davina Heald Foundation, makers of Denial and Avoidance, has collapsed. The company has been dogged for some months by accusations that its products were dangerous. Critics have claimed that Denial is linked to dangerous ingredients such as 'self-confidence', 'self-esteem' and 'inner peace' that have been conclusively proven to lead to marital breakdown, loss of employment and other major dramatic changes in people's lives. Beauty experts have been quick to seize on this news and to claim that pentapeptides are much more interesting.

USA Brand spokesman for Denial, OJ Simpson said ...

The Future's History

[The following is an excerpt from the book 'The Future's History'. In this book, a radical UK Prime Minister, Purvis McEwen, is elected and decides to redress the inaccurate reporting of history by having people attend government-approved 'History Centres' to record their stories.

In the first wave of those to be recorded is Julian Rich, a young man living in Cardiff who has a terrible secret, a secret that he decides that he needs to share with his girlfriend before he tells the government].

Julian stirred his cup of coffee and looked out of the window idly. There was Jane running down the street past the library, late as ever. He had had a few moments to think about what he would say to her at least. There she was now, she was telling the woman at the door who was trying to hand her a menu, that she was going to come over and sit with her ... pause ... then she is led over.

"Sorry," said Jane, pulling out a chair and sitting opposite him.

"Are you ready to order?" asked the woman with a name badge that identified her as Harmony.

"I don't know," said Jane, flustered, "I fancy some chicken."

"You're in Nando's, that doesn't help," said Julian flatly.

"Maybe just a drink for now, I'm running a bit late, coffee thank you, Harmony."

"You order at the counter, Madam," replied Harmony abruptly before walking away.

"Look, sorry Jules, sorry, sorry, I have had a mad morning. You needed to speak to me?"

"Yes, but don't worry, I have had time to sit here and reflect."

"Reflect on what?" asked Jane, sounding worried.

"Relationships. Isn't it odd? When you're 15 you love to use the word boyfriend - or girlfriend for me - then at 25 it is a bit of an awkward word but manfriend is a bit weird and partner a bit formal. Then at 35 you really are stuck, aren't you? I could see you there at the door. Harmony tried to seat you somewhere and you said oh no, you were with your ... pause. Boyfriend? Partner?"

"Sure," said Jane, playing with the salt and pepper shakers and not really looking at him, "I suppose so. At 15 you want a wild, radical rebel though. At 35 you want someone with a steady job who is not going to blow it all on a motorbike."

"You ought to get yourself a drink."

Jane walked over to the counter while Julian watched her. They had been together a year now, mostly happy, mostly staying in each other's houses, mostly appreciating that they were mortgage-paying house people with steady jobs. Everything was really quite, quite normal ... except for the thing that he was about to tell her.

Every relationship has a secret that one person thinks might kill everything dead. This was Julian's. This, he imagined, was this relationship's.

Jane bought a refillable fizzy drink, of course. He knew her orders by now and probably should have ordered for her - is that sexist, he was never sure? The choices in Nando's were pretty consistent, he had this crazy idea of a waiter emerging from the kitchen and shouting 'okay then, who ordered the chicken?' Still, on a wet Tuesday lunchtime there was hardly much competition for seats.

Jane sat her fizzy drink down heavily on the table. She smiled a slightly nervous and expectant smile. She too had plans for this relationship, but she was attentive to the possibility of the killer fact that would strangle it early on. She had a few facts of her own kept in reserve.

"I have something to tell you," said Julian, stirring what was left of his coffee.

"Go on," said Jane, not making eye contact.

"Okay, you may not like this, but I love you and I want us to have a future together, a future that we can both be happy in. This bloody government thing, they'll make me say everything and I think that I need to be honest ... there's something I haven't told you. There's ... err ... a secret that I haven't told you. Something I've been doing for a while now, something that you are not going to like."

"I know," Jane said softly, reaching a hand over to hold Julian's.

"You do? Why ... I mean, how?"

"It's been pretty obvious for a while. There are times when you won't see me, times when you go out and won't tell me where you're going. I know what you are."

"You do? Wow, I don't know what to say," said Julian, excited and relieved at his ... girlfriend's ... loving reaction. This was not what he expected.

"It's all right darling," she said, stroking his hand gently, "I know that you're a Conservative voter. I forgive you."

"What? No! That's not it!"

"You're not a Tory? I could have sworn you did leafletting and everything," replied Jane, sitting back and removing her hand from his.

"Yes, I am. But that's not it. That's not what I'm ashamed to tell you."

"It should be - you should see what they are doing to this country, to Wales especially. Did you know that youth unemployment ..."

"Stop, no, that's not what I want to talk about. There's something else, something worse."

"Believe me lover, there's nothing worse than being a Tory!" said Jane, now looking around to see if anyone could hear their conversation. She took a slurp from her drink and waited for him to continue.

"Okay, okay, no, it's not politics. There's another reason why I can't see you sometimes.

I'm ...," and here Julian took a gulp from his own drink, "... a werewolf."

"A what?"

"A werewolf, one of an ancient order of creatures. Have you ever noticed that about once a month, I can't be around you? It's because I turn into this kind of monster."

"Yeah, well I do that some months too ... but ... you mean that you go out at night and drink blood?"

"No, that's vampires. They don't exist, they're mythical creatures."

"Like werewolves?"

"No, werewolves exist. I am one. Vampires do not exist. They are made up."

Jane sat back in her chair and stared at him for a while. She held her drink at the right angle to send a chunky ice cube down the glass into her mouth. She crunched on it suspiciously. Eventually she spoke again.

"You always were quite hairy."

"It's not actually just hairy people, you know."

"Do you have a wolf pack then?"

"Yes, I do. Some of the guys I hang around with, they are werewolves too. Andy, Steve ..."

"I'll bet that John Herrian is. His palms are hairy as hell."

"He's not and it's not about the hair and ... hey, how do you know how hairy he is?"

Jane looked around the restaurant and then lowered her voice. "Look, if this is some kind of kinky sex game, that's fine. I'm in my 30s, this is the last time to do this kind of thing before the kids come along. Sure, you can be a hairy beast if you want to, just don't let's set this up in some chicken place."

Julian buried his head in his hands and then swallowed hard. This was proving harder than he had imagined and he had imagined it being hard.

"This is not about kinky sex, I ..."

"Hold on, you're saying no vampires. I saw the Twilight movies years ago. If you have vampires, you have werewolves. You can't tell me that there's one and not the other."

"Vampires were made up by Bram Stoker. They are fictional."

"And werewolves. Vampires and werewolves have always been enemies. They're like sports teams that don't get on - Cardiff City and Swansea City or the Scarlets rugby team and just about anyone else in the known world. I get it, men like to be in packs, don't we know it!"

There was a silence and Julian studied his nails (not hairy) to avoid eye contact. Dammit, everyone asked about the hair. This was not the first relationship that he had been rocked by his news. Jane was still looking at him suspiciously. She had lovely blue eyes. She was dressed smartly for her office job too, a look that he liked. Her face was scanning his for any inclination that he was making an elaborate joke but finding none.

"Okay," she said, moving the cutlery between them out of the way, "so you go out and drink blood in cemeteries ..."

"Well, we run free in the field beyond Cefn Mably - it's an unknown Victorian law that every local Council has to provide space for werewolves to run ... we got a Prime Minister back in ..."

"Can I kill you with a stake?"

"No. Well, yes, obviously if you put a stake into most people's hearts you will kill them."

"So, I am right!" said Jane, looking rather pleased with herself, "Hey that's a joke - where does a vampire never eat? A steakhouse!"

Jane laughed at her own joke far more than anyone else would. To be honest, she had heard worse revelations than this. Julian had his head in his hands again. He did look a bit wolf-like, she thought. She had always thought that he should have shaved his back, perhaps this is why they had argued about that. She had always objected to the way that he stirred pasta, perhaps this is why they had argued about that.

"Do you have any questions for me?" he asked, observing her thoughtful silence, "I can tell you anything – history, how I found out, pack behaviour ... anything at all about what I have told you here today."

"I do have one question,"

"Go ahead."

"It's about my aunt. You know Aunt Sarah, out in Maerdy. Well, she's disabled, of course, as you saw. Now my question is this, right. She had her disabled living allowance taken away and she can barely afford to eat every day. How can you vote for a government that targeted the most vulnerable in such a disgusting manner?"

Julian shook his head in exasperation, "No, I mean questions about being a werewolf!"

His voice was loud enough now that other people briefly looked up from their chicken dishes to see what the noise was. Julian took a deep breath and composed himself. It was not quite how he had imagined 'coming out' would be.

Jane thought for a moment and imagined going back to work. The younger girls at work were always talking about men, perhaps she could now say that she was dating 'a real animal'. Work ... she paused and looked around, her lunch break would not last much longer.

"We should talk about this tonight," she said.

Julian sighed and agreed. He did not feel that the conversation had really taken them very far, but she did at least seem to be taking the news in good humour.

"Come on," she said, "I'll walk you back. Oh yes – was your ex-wife a werewolf too?"

Julian paused as he rose from the table, he was always uncertain about any mention of his previous marriage. So often the questions about it came from an agenda that he had not seen and now he looked for it but could not find it.

"No ... no, she wasn't."

Jane grabbed his arm and cuddled into him. He left some money on the table and they walked out together.

"Come on," said Jane playfully, "maybe tonight I'll let you drink my blood or something!"

Julian did not answer as they walked back past the library towards the city centre. In his mind he was muttering, 'No, it's vampires who drink blood and ... THEY DON'T EXIST!'

"Hey Harm," called the other waitress watching the giggling couple as they walked away from the restaurant, "Good tippers?"

"No, lousy," said Harmony sadly picking up the money from the table, "only had two drinks anyway."

Harmony pondered the couple. "You know Den, I think that he was the low tipper. I think that I would have got more from his ... what **do** you call it at that age?"

Eng-ger-Land Land

"Yes, but **why** do we have to stop here?"

It was the unmistakable voice of a teenager sitting in the back of a car while her parents talked in the front. Mr Morgan turned around from the passenger side to face his daughter.

"You know that we are going to stop here, we talked about it before we set out."

Celyn turned to look out of the window at the rain-sodden hills. She had used up her store of 'it's not fair!'s some years ago and now she only had to make a sulking face for her father to know that it was not fair and that Carys's parents would never have put her through this. She had heard a rumour that Carys's parents were going to let her go to Manchester for her 17th birthday. Carys's parents were the example of everything that parents should be. It was so strange that Carys said that she hated them.

"We saw this place on the news," called out her mother unhelpfully from the front seat, "they've set up some kind of theme park for tourists and we thought that we would stop."

"But it's miles to Aberystwyth, we won't be there before it's dark!"

"We won't stop long, you might like it if you try."

"I won't," replied Celyn to both the idea of liking and the idea of trying.

* * * * *

"And if it hadn't been for us coming in and taking over, there might not be a Post Office here," Mrs J. Carol Brown was telling Mr and Mrs Morgan and their daughter, who was convinced that the woman had called her Kevin, "Trouble is, everyone commutes nowadays and it is quite hard to sustain a business in a small town like this. That's when we hit on the theme park idea."

Only fifteen minutes before, J. Carol Brown had been wiping down plastic table coverings with a scouring sponge. Visitors were welcome.

"We have even got the name in Welsh there- that's pretty impressive, eh? It rhymes as well in Welsh too – *Tost a Post* – clever, eh?"

"We're on our way to Aberystwyth," explained Mr Morgan rather needlessly, "I had heard about your theme park from the TV news."

"Ah yes, we were on Look North West two weeks ago."

The Morgan parents looked at each other, not quite sure whether they had been watching BBC Wales last week or not. Their daughter understood things before they did.

"It's the Manchester news, Mam, she lives in Wales and doesn't watch Welsh news."

"Yes well," said Mrs Brown a little awkwardly, "when we retired here we wanted to keep up with things back home."

Mr and Mrs Morgan smiled, their daughter scowled. The small talk had gone far enough for now, so the family made their way to a recently-wiped plastic-topped table and sat down.

"Maybe just some tea and a cake?" suggested Mrs Morgan.

A man emerged from the back of the kitchen. Celyn put him in that age bracket of 60-100 years old that only teenagers think exist. She noticed his bright green cardigan and his beard but his jolly manner had brought him over to their table before she could make any more judgements.

"Hello, I'm Roger," he announced with a pleasure that betrayed how few customers had been in that day.

"We normally stop in Dolgellau," explained Mr Morgan as if he could continue the conversation that he had had with the woman he presumed to be Roger's wife, "but we saw on the news the item about this new .. err ... thing opening in Llanrwst, so we thought we'd stop."

"Well, we're not quite open yet," said Roger, stroking his beard, "but you can certainly have a look around. Easter for the Grand Opening. Quite a party planned. Get the folks coming down from the coast – it's less than fifteen miles."

"Ten miles," corrected Celyn insistently.

"Well, it doesn't matter really, does it?" replied Mrs Morgan brushing her daughter's hand to show that she should keep quiet. It was probably at least ten years too late for that action to have had any effect.

"But it did matter," said Celyn with more insistence, "the point is that Llanrwst is ten miles away from Conwy. When the Normans built their castle in Conwy they banned the Welsh from coming within ten miles of it and that is why the town of Llanrwst developed exactly ten miles from the castle."

Mrs Morgan smiled at Roger Brown as if to say 'daughters, eh?' and Mr Brown smiled back, though he had no children of his own.

"I'm sure that it was necessary, Kelly," said Mrs J. Carol Brown, appearing behind her husband hastily, "the English were bringing their way of life to the area, they didn't want that to be threatened. Now, Roger will take your order, won't you dear?"

"Of course, what can we treat you to today?"

"I think that we'll all have tea and some of that chocolate cake – Cel, do you want lemonade? No, okay, we'll have tea and cake for three."

"Great choice!" said Roger, which seemed a little out of place in a café in Snowdonia, then he scurried back into the kitchen.

The comfortable silence did not last long.

"It's wrong you know," said Celyn, "*Tost a Post* – it should be *Tost a Phost*. I think that it was written by someone who didn't realise that both *tost* and *post* rhyme with 'frost' and not 'boast'".

"You don't have to correct everyone, dear."

"Are you excited about your work experience?" asked Mr Morgan to try to save the conversation.

"'Spose," was Celyn's answer.

They sat in silence again until the pots of tea arrived, all presented in delicate china on a gold-coloured tray. Being the only customers led to a certain kind of privilege.

Mrs Morgan was a proud mother and she could not resist a little boast.

"My daughter's going down to Cardiff to do work experience with the BBC."

"Oh really?" said Roger, knowing that he had to be suitably impressed, "a career in the media for you then?"

"I already have my own radio show on the school station in Amlwch," said Celyn without much emotion.

"Amlwch?" asked Roger, "Ah yes, Anglesey. Carol and I did look there when we first retired. I say retired – look at how we're working now! Yes, strangely flat Anglesey. Weird, you don't expect Wales to be flat really. Amlwch – right at the tip?"

"That's right," confirmed Mr Morgan.

"Well, if you get into the BBC, tell them to remember that there are people in North Wales too, won't you?" said Roger with a smile to show that it was intended as light teasing.

"I run my own radio show," repeated Celyn, "*Holi Celyn* – it's kind of a pun because *holi* means ask and *Celyn* means Holly. You see, *Holi* Celyn and ... it's an advice show ... and ..."

Roger was staring patiently but with no sign of following what the teenager was talking about so she stopped talking. He smiled and wished them a good tea and cake before leaving them in some kind of peace.

"Why must you do that?" asked the mother.

"Do what?" was the challenge.

"Be so difficult with people!"

"I'm not difficult. Not my fault he can't understand a bilingual pun. I'll bet they are like those newspaper editors who demand that immigrants to England be made to speak English but who will one day retire to Gwynedd and get annoyed when people want to speak Welsh."

"You shouldn't be so judgemental."

Celyn shrugged and said no more. Mr Morgan had pulled out the map and was looking at their route down the A470 and making sure that he knew when to tell his wife to turn west towards Aberystwyth.

The tea and cake were eaten in a truce of a silence. Celyn looked at the rain out of the window and longed to be in Aberystwyth again. It seemed stupid and she would never dare tell her parents this, but ever since she had been a child, that first view of the sweep of the seafront from the bottom of Pier Street had enchanted her. She lived by the sea yes, but Aberystwyth was proper seaside to her, the seaside of piers and terraces and fish and chips and ice cream and these holiday trips.

However, she was certainly not going to let on anything like that to her parents and she stabbed her piece of chocolate cake with her fork belligerently.

After a while, the Browns came back and asked if the Morgans would still like to see the newsworthy set-up in the background. 'Why, yes' was the polite answer, ''Spose' was the impolite answer.

Mr Brown took up the story as they made their way to the back of the property –

"We had all this land out the back. You'd be amazed what you can afford in Wales – well, compared to Manchester, but anyway ... we always wanted to do something about it. We wanted an attraction to bring people here."

"The forests and the river and the ancient bridge not enough?" asked Celyn.

"Indeed not, we needed something to draw people in and it was then that I thought ..."

"**I** thought," interrupted J. Carol Brown, "It was one day over the kitchen table, when we were discussing the business. I said 'what about your English friend, Dai?'"

"And I said that Dai is not particularly English."

"And I said 'well he has to be, that is why they call him 'English Dai'!"

41

Mr Morgan coughed abruptly to jolt the Browns out of their back and forth reverie.

"Ah yes," said Mr Brown, "Carol said that Dai goes over to Benidorm to eat fish 'n' chips, sit on the beach with an ice cream, drink English beer and then watch the FA Cup final in the pub. What he wants is England, but abroad."

"So we thought," continued his wife excited by her own ideas, "Why not create that here – so we have constructed 'Englandland' ... or perhaps 'EnglandWorld'."

"I'd go with Englandland," muttered Celyn.

At this point they walked into the field at the back of the property. The Browns seemed suddenly animated and the Morgans started to recognise what they had seen on the news the week before. Everything was shut and dark of course, but they could imagine it full of light and tourists.

"Over here is the English pub- we'll have Boddingtons and all the English ales on tap of course and proper food like Yorkshire pub and roast beef too. Then you have a pier-like design there for amusement arcades – the machines aren't there yet ... and we're hoping to put sand along there for a beach."

"So long as it doesn't rain," observed Mr Morgan, only too aware of how many of their trips to Aberystwyth had needed rainy day plans.

"Oh yes ... oh yes," said Roger walking to the other side of the field, "Scuse the walkways, still need to have the paths done. We had wanted a whole funfair but the planning permission was a nightmare. Bloody Council, no sympathy. Yes, anyway, over here is the fish n chip bar and a bar with wall to wall TVs only showing football."

The Morgans watched as he jumped from place to place. He walked back to them saying, "We wanted an English cricket pitch or somewhere for Morris Dancers but would your average English bloke in here for the football want to watch some dancing?"

"English culture is just too rich," sighed Mrs J. Carol Brown, "but I do think that we have caught something here. What do you think? Just like Benidorm, you can go on holiday but bring the best of England with you. English newspapers and things are easy of course, what do you think?"

"I think that it is very ... interesting," said Mr Morgan, using that wonderful English word that gives no condemnation and no praise.

The Browns smiled, thinking that it was praise.

* * * * *

The Morgans drove on to Aberystwyth, initially in silence. Mrs Morgan could use the satnav, but it was part of her relationship with her husband that he wrestled with a huge map while she pondered turning left or right. They had driven this way many times, but it was part of their ritual.

"I don't know why you have such a problem with them."

Mr Morgan was talking out loud and looking forwards. He would not normally have commented, but everyone in the car knew who he was addressing. His daughter said nothing and looked out of the window at the trees passing by.

"They're actually doing something, you know. If you want to work in the media you are going to have to learn about something called subjectivity."

"*Dw i'n gwybod ...* I know what that means, Dad."

"Don't you admire someone running their own business?"

"No. They are taking. They have bought up cheap property that could have been bought by someone local. They are encouraging people to come over and have an 'experience' rather than actually understanding the language or culture of the country that they are visiting. They are little better than the Mancunians who come over to the caravan parks with their own packed lunches, take a good lungful of seaside air and return back to the city without actually spending any money."

Mr Morgan turned around to look at his daughter directly. Mrs Morgan glanced over at him nervously.

"It's all the same with your generation ..."

"Steven!" said Mrs Morgan to try to stop him.

"And what has your generation done?"

"Celyn Haf Morgan! You stop your chopsing right now!"

Celyn shrugged and look out of the window but her father, perhaps not realising that he had some years of these conversations to go through yet, could not avoid continuing.

"Your generation. You all want to be angry and irritated. You want to criticise everything. Everything is wrong, everything is against you. But what do you do? What do you do to make anything of your own?"

"Dad, I'm only a teenager, if you two got off my back ..."

"You're even going to Cardiff. Cardiff! What happens then? You go off to University somewhere, get a job, settle down ..."

"I don't want any of your future for me."

"Settle down and never come back. What is there at home for you? But what are you doing to change that? Those people, they may be idiots – I am not completely convinced that they are not - but they are doing something. All you want to do is complain, how about actually doing something?"

Celyn looked out the window and her father turned back around to look out the front of the car. The engine hummed, the trees passed by, finally Mrs Morgan spoke.

"Steven, be a darling and check the road that goes down to Machnynlleth."

In the back of the car, Celyn muttered 'it's so unfair'. In the front of the car, her father mouthed 'Carys's parents would have let her do it'.

45

Me, I'm Legend, I am

It is an odd thing to look back on the great calamity that befell the human race in 2015 and realise that most of us in Wales reacted by calmly waiting for a replacement bus service.

I was off work when it happened – skiving, mitching, pulling a sickie, call it what you will, I had been fed up and decided to take a day away from my job – writing press releases and policy statements for a charity in Cardiff. I had worked hard enough to deserve one, I thought. As it was, this one bit of laziness led me to miss the day when the human race finally stared disaster in the face. While panic spread across parts of England, I was snuggled up in my duvet and blankets dreaming of ice cream on the beach with Alison Tokwith from HR.

The great irony is that having spent the day in my little Vale of Glamorgan village, I am now being asked to record the events in far away cities that day and the destruction that followed. I will tell you what I know.

'The apocalypse started on a wet Thursday evening ...'

It was a Thursday when I took my sickie and I am told that the first signs involved a number of meteorite strikes on earth. We had watched enough films to know that this was possible but never thought that they would strike major capitals at the same time. I am told that in the wake of these strikes, the wifi signal disappeared. Of course, in the semi-rural Vale the reaction to losing wifi signal was, 'what, again?' and a resigned sigh.

What do you do? Ring a call centre in India where they ask you if you have tried switching everything off and turning it back on again? In what was left of London they were running around desperately pressing phone buttons, but we continued as normal.

I am told that no-one knew where the meteors had come from (meteors? Meteorites? I have been told to make sure that all my words are correct). However, panic spread through London, Edinburgh, Paris, Rome ... but not Cardiff, Cardiff was still there and I went to the train station as normal on Friday to wait for my train in to Cardiff for work. Had someone told me that a global catastrophe was unfolding on the other side of the Severn, I would never have been so worried about having taken the day off.

If there was someone behind the chaos that followed, they understood that human-beings had two weaknesses. The first was our love of communication – heck, we knew that, whenever the Americans invaded some small, defenceless country they would first take out the mobile phone network. Perhaps someone just copied them? The mobile networks cut out while I was on the phone to a friend travelling from Carmarthen to Lampeter. Once again, we were lucky in Wales – as panic ensued across Europe (and further), in Wales I just shrugged my shoulders because you always lose signal somewhere in Carmarthenshire.

Our other weakness was that there were so many of us and those cities that we had built were like hives where we met and interacted with hundreds of people a day. A communicable disease that was introduced into that mix ... again, this is really no different to when the Spanish arrived in South America and wiped out the Aztecs by bringing them smallpox. I need to stop doing that, I was told to keep this account factual and avoid my opinions. Let me put it this way, even with my A-level history, I know that we were vulnerable.

By the weekend, I was annoyed that the TV was not working. Cardiff City were playing away and that was my only hope for highlights – little did I realise that the team had found the airport closed and the Severn Bridge blocked as police moved to try to stop people travelling around. There was chaos over in England, apparently. For me? Yes, the Spar shop in the village ran out of pies and could not order more, that caused some panic, but largely things continued as normal at first.

I suppose that when I reflect on it, we were not conditioned to things running perfectly so we were always able to adapt. You know what it is like – the transport network broke down and I arrived at the station to find a sign saying that there would be no trains. I imagined that there was a points failure or a freight train derailment and went to wait for the rail replacement bus service. In the queue we complained about privatisation and the cost of travel these days, but otherwise we simply waited. Nothing ever came. That had happened to me a few times before too.

I am told that elsewhere in the UK, rioting had broken out by Monday and many of our senior politicians and officials went into hiding or simply fled. Power networks started to break down and it emerged that serious fighting had broken out further east. Fearing a nuclear attack, Russia had invaded Eastern Europe and China had invaded Russia. Generals in charge of large forces who had planned for invasions found no civilian authorities to override their actions. I was still worrying about disciplinary action over that sickie. There was still a queue at the station the next morning for the replacement bus.

I have been told that I need to write more quickly, so here is a speeded up version of what happened next. Yes, in Wales we did have some trouble with English people trying to make it across the border. News of the disease that they brought with them meant that many were turned away and an effective barrier was mounted around much of the north-east and Powys while further south the bridges were blocked. We organised ourselves in Welsh – my GCSE grade 'B' in the language just about getting me by at first – so that the newcomers were not aware of what we were doing (the irony is that they used to claim we were doing that anyway, but now we needed to do it).

The army arrived in my village and announced that they were in charge, The world's population had apparently been devastated and the decision had been made to take the survivors from Wales to all those conference venues across Mid Wales until the crisis was over. It made sense, people had started fleeing the village looking for relatives and I had heard that this was true across much of the country. Rural, west and north Wales had largely been unaffected but we needed to gather together to prepare for whatever was coming next and to prepare to fight if we needed to do so.

Arriving at the former Girlguiding headquarters at Broneirion, I said that I had worked in Communications. '*Archeddog*' ... sorry, I was told that I had to write in English, 'Excellent' had been the response of Commander Barry who put me in charge of trying to keep a record of what had happened. Every day I would be briefed and every day I would record how the human race survived, presuming that we would do so for future generations.

As I write, I can hear the voice of the Commander, asking how I am doing. I am probably done for now. We are moving an expeditionary force out towards what was once Birmingham tomorrow to see what else is there. The suspicion is that whoever or whatever has caused this has left England and Scotland pretty much devastated.

Keep writing in English, the Commander tells me, we now have so few people who only speak English that we need to do what we can to keep the language alive.

Then he pauses and looks unsure as to whether he should share what he knows. I try to pull an innocent face because I am intrigued. I know that he has been pondering the same question that we have all pondered- why us? Why have so many in Wales survived when so much else has been devastated by whatever or whoever has happened?

"You know," he says in Welsh, "if this is the work of someone either on earth or not on earth, we may have an idea what they are doing. We found this."

He throws me a copy of a UK government 'welcome to the United Kingdom' brochure. It was clearly intended for people coming to live here. I flick through all the charming, unrealistic pictures of village postboxes and rolling hills. I shake my head as I cannot see what he sees as so significant. He points to the first sentence –

"The United Kingdom is a union of the kingdoms of England and Scotland."

He shrugs.

"Maybe they read this and never realised we existed."

Ten Top Tips for Using Facebook

When a very good friend of mine joined Facebook after many years of opting out of the social media world, I wrote the following helpful guide for him. I was struck by his comment that he 'didn't want to make any mistakes' and thought that I would put together ten handy hints on how to survive in this online environment -

1) Facebook is a fun and easy way to communicate and no-one is pedantic enough to worry about things like spelling and grammar. The important thing about social media is communication so feel free to use 'could of', 'your' instead of 'you're' and 'affect' rather than 'effect' and no-one will be tedious enough to point this out.

2) The number of Friends you have on Facebook is a measure of your personal worth. People with over 1000 Friends are worth knowing, ignore people with 74 Friends.

3) On the Privacy Settings menu, remember to tick the box 'Share all my information with the US government'. It is for your own protection.

4) If you have an event in your life, remember to take at least 400 photos and upload them all for everyone to see. If some have come out blurry or unusable then upload them as well because people will enjoy scrolling through all of them. This goes double for baby photos or photos from your holidays.

5) When looking for a photo for your profile, be sure to get someone else to take it so that you have a good picture. You will not find any photos of people with one arm outstretched to hold the camera. Taking a lot of photos of yourself is frowned on.

6) Find yourself on a night out? It is important to take photos of everyone involved, preferably using a mobile phone held shakily, and then tag them all on Facebook. If they object, no worries, tag them anyway as no-one seriously objects to you uploading photos of them without their permission.

7) People love to hear about the trivial things you do in your life, especially if you add the magic letters 'LOL'. Forget boring stuff like birth, death, marriage and your thoughts about life, concentrate your Status on important things like 'Just bought some cornflakes LOL!!!!!' - remember that the more exclamation marks you use, the more interesting the update will be.

8) Everyone loves the Facebook Timeline.

9) Why not Friend all the people that you work with? It is a cool way to keep in contact with your workplace. Make sure your Line Manager is Friended especially, they will find it really funny when you fail to turn up at work and your Status reads 'can't be arsed so taking a sickie'.

10) Remember that Facebook is not serious. If people become stroppy or difficult with you, they are only pretending. After all, they have never met you, so how could they be upset by what you

write? If someone does start threatening you, send them your name and address and invite them to come to your house to talk it over in person.

Enjoy your time online!

The End of Everything

"And what they' singin'

Back to back, belly to belly,

I don't give a damn, 'cause I done dead already

Back to back, belly to belly,

At the zombie jamboree."

Phil Ellis and I had three things in common. Before meeting unexpectedly in the middle of Queen Street last week, we had not seen each other for nearly ten years. We had been the best of friends at school - best friends that is until Phil left suddenly - and those school days were the first thing I shared with the man now jumping on the sofa, singing enthusiastically to the record while all the time carefully trying not to spill the glass of whisky in his left hand.

This activity had confirmed to me that my old best friend was single. An adult male who jumps on a sofa is always single. The few who are not single soon find that preserving the furniture is one of those unwritten wedding vows that their wives may seem to take as seriously as all the love, honour and cherish proclamations.

"I can't believe that we both ..." he exclaimed breathlessly as the needle reached the centre of the record.

Caribbean folk music – that would be the second thing. We had both had a curious taste in music as teenagers - I still had my copy of ELO's "Out of the Blue" and was saddened when Phil told me he gave his to a charity shop years ago. Now boxes of Caribbean folk formed little islands across the front room of his flat in Roath. There was not much space and these old boxes, to a man who had been married and remained firmly cynical, cried out for a woman to say 'But anyone could fall over them there!' Phil was definitely single, loved his Caribbean folk and frequently aroused the wrath of Roath with it (not least because he insisted on vinyl records rather than CDs or internet streaming). What about the third thing we have in common?

"Tim. Tim," said Phil wiping away the sweat from his forehead, "I am so pleased to have bumped into you again. I know ... I know I haven't kept in touch with any of our school mates, but ..."

Phil sat down heavily on the sofa where he had moments ago been dancing to Zombie Jamboree. He swept a hand through his thinning hair and creased his reddened face into a smile. He looked at ease with the world, which is why I brought up that third thing - personal tragedy.

"Phil ..." I started cautiously, "Do you ever think about Emma Harris?"

Phil swallowed the rest of his whisky in one gulp and strode towards the bottle for a re-fill. He steadily poured himself a careful measure and then spoke as if every word was a footstep across an emotional high-wire.

"For a long time I did, Tim, for a long time I did. At first, well, you'll remember how distraught I was. I blamed myself so much for her death. For four ... maybe five years, I spent so much time depressed about it that it was as if my life ... stopped ... as well as hers."

A frown now creased his face and I noticed how his body sagged at the seams of his sweatshirt. I nervously sipped at my vodka and tonic. It had been the question I had been dying to ask. As a seventeen year old he had been crazy about Emma and I think that she had quite liked him too. Then one night she drove over to his house - she thought they were going out for a meal, but his parents were on holiday and he had other plans. They drank and talked for a while and then he 'made his move' as we used to say. Emma was so taken aback that she ran out and drove off in her car. The car hit a tree … and, well, Phil …

Phil had been distraught. Even his closest friends only saw him once or twice before his parents decided to pack up and move away to spare their son any more reminders of the tragedy. You can imagine that seeing him back in Cardiff ten years later had shocked me quite profoundly. I had imagined him suicidal or regretfully working on in some dull job never to get over the loss. In fact, when my wife died I think that maybe I even comforted myself with the thought of his misfortune.

"But you know what changed me - when you told me yesterday about how your wife died, I was reminded of this. Five years later, I was trying to get my life back together. I was in bed with this woman from Swindon. Can't even remember her name now ... but I remember she was from Swindon ... sad that ..." he continued, resting back on the sofa again, "And we were asleep in bed one night and she suddenly screams and swears. Naturally I'm awake immediately, yelling 'What's wrong, what's wrong?'. And you know what, she woke up and found that she had broken a fingernail. That was the tragedy. And suddenly, in a wave, the true trivial nature of the world descended on me and I realised that there was just no point in mourning any more. In this life there are people who want to be happy and people who are only happy when they have got something to complain about. I was fed up with being in the latter category. Yes, life is unfair but I want to enjoy what I can, despite that."

I stared at him rather blankly. Since Lucy died ... but Phil interrupted my thoughts with a sudden burst of animation.

"Here, I've got a recording of Island Woman you should hear. Ah ... making me forget, a-who I am ... yeah, I'll put this one on for you. Pass me that glass, there's some more tonic in the fridge if you need it. Oh and don't be fooled by the sportswear, I'm still deeply unfit."

And so that was about as deep as the conversation had gone. I was disappointed in Phil in some ways - we shared tragedy in our lives and whereas I felt the sorrow of the loss of Lucy every day, he seemed to be living as if nothing had happened. How could that bouncy, happy grown-up man be the miserable teenager who had moved cities to escape his past? What would Emma think if she could see him with his own business, seeing other women as well?

Later that afternoon, I walked towards home with this annoyance starting to build in me. When I turned into Queen's Street I approached the spot where a voice had cried out 'Tim! Tim Hendy! My God, Tim! It's me, Phil!' what seemed like an eternity ago now ... pushing past the shoppers, their faces not even registering in my mind, I headed down the road towards home. It was great to see him again but why did he annoy me now?

And that was when I saw her. She laughed and said, "Hello Tim."

I stopped short and stared. I straightened my jacket and breathed in slightly. There were no marks on her, no signs of the cancer that had killed her, a rare smile on her face. Yes, all in all, even the most cynical observer would have to say that my former wife (or was she still my wife?) looked pretty good for a dead girl.

"I'll bet you're thinking that I look pretty good for a dead girl, aren't you?" she said playfully.

"No, no ..." I stammered.

"There're no carbohydrates in eternity, that's the secret."

The pause seemed to last longer than anything. The Saturday shoppers pushed past us with their bright bags and unhappy faces, but I did not notice any of it. Eventually I spoke - let me tell you now, I had never had that much eloquence with attractive living girls, but dead ones seemed to kill off my powers of speech completely.

"So ... err ... are you actually dead?" I asked, proving to myself exactly what I meant about losing eloquence.

"Hmm ... let me see now, am I dead?" she mused sarcastically, "Well I do sort of remember having a serious illness somewhere along the line ... treatment, scans ... hmm ... oh yes, something's coming back to me ... a hospital, my heart stopping - yes, I think that the part where I actually died would have been the clue on that one."

A shopper knocked her to one side with a full bag of groceries. She laughed as the flustered old woman apologised. It seemed to be proof that other people could see her too. I pinched myself. It hurt. I tried to think of an explanation for this incredible event. It hurt.

"I never liked your sarcasm. But, please ... there's so much I need to know. Like, when did you come back ... what's going on ... err ..."

"Do you still live in Cyncoed?" she asked.

"No ... no, I stayed on there for a while after ... for a while after ... but then I got this flat in Riverside - I was just walking back there. Phil Ellis lives here again you know, he lives in Roath. Why ... err ... why don't you come back and tell me about everything?"

Not the most well-delivered of suggestions, but it was about as close to sensible as I could manage after such a shock. And so, me and my dead wife, we walked towards the Castle. It is amazing how easy it is for people to fit back on to the rails that they previously rolled down. Just as years ago, before she became ill, I started to try to make Lucy value me, to get beyond those sarcastic assumptions and irksome little put-downs that had taken her over in those last months.

"I've been promoted at the Tourist Board," I boasted.

"What happened to being a cartoonist?"

"Oh I never got that far. But we've got some great campaigns going. 'Cardiff - the perfect place for anything' is the theme that we're ..."

"Hey, can I see my gravestone?" she interrupted with sudden excitement.

"I had you cremated."

"Why the hell did you do that? I mean, the heat ... remember when I got so burnt in Majorca? And you go and bloody burn me again. Well, thanks a lot!"

We carried on in silence, just as we always had done. Then, just past the animal wall, she turned to me and motioned me to stop. There was a resigned look on her face.

"I'm sorry. I always did that, didn't I? You're going to create great campaigns and I'm worried about being burnt. Being dead these last five years - well, it's been odd. One moment I was drifting off in hospital and you were crying your eyes out you poor lamb. Then I had five years of eternity and then, last week, well I found myself back on earth. I seem to move, eat, sleep and do all the other things. I've even met quite a few others, though mostly in Cardiff. It's scary. It's exciting. I don't know how to handle it. I never meant to be so negative. So take me back to your pad and introduce me as your ex-wife in the realest sense. I just want to enjoy myself," she explained solemnly. Then with a laugh she added, "Just don't believe anyone when they tell you that you're a long time dead!"

We walked back to Riverside more amicably. I gave her news of all that had changed over the last five years. She was pleased to hear that Cardiff Arms Park had been demolished and then sad to hear that it had been replaced with the Millennium Stadium. I don't know if she was joking when she said there was no rugby in the afterlife. It certainly made it sound like paradise. She was ... well, much the same, if a little kinder and friendlier. I stopped remembering her as the ill woman I had seen die in hospital and began to think of her as that lively dark-haired woman I met at University. Her only disappointment was that I had not re-married.

"Why not?" she asked.

"Well, no-one could replace you."

"Oh don't give me that rubbish. I don't want you to find someone to replace me. I want you to find someone to keep you company and make you happy. I'm dead. I'm never going to come back - present situation excepted. It's time to move on - did you never see 'Truly, Madly, Deeply'?"

"Frankly, this is all a bit too much 'The Sixth Sense' for me."

"Is that one of those sci-fi things I never watched?"

"It was ... sort of, you should see it while you're here. It's about this lad who ... err ... he, well, he sees dead people. I was going to say that it was all rather unbelievable."

She drank in the walk back to the flat, all the new sites and sounds of the city nourishing her interest. Once we were back at the flat, I decided that I had to make a phone call so I put the kettle on while Lucy surveyed some of the same old furnishings she had left all those years ago. And one person's name stood out in my mind if I was going to phone a friend.

"Phil? Yes, it's me, Tim. You are not going to believe this. Something, something unbelievable has happened. I don't know how to handle it ... I ... okay, I'm calming down ..."

In the background I heard Phil's doorbell ring (it played the first line of 'Guide Me O Thou Great Redeemer') and after a little apology he went to see who it was. Maybe I was impatient because my news was so important, maybe I felt selfish because I wanted my news to be more important than his visitor, whoever it was. I felt as though he took ten minutes to answer the door. I could hear voices, one high-pitched and Phil's calm tones sounding rather harassed and unsure. When he came back to the phone, his voice seemed unable to grip hold of the words that he wanted to use.

"Sorry Tim, I'm so sorry, I've got to go. I really have to go and deal with this first."

"Phil, what the hell is going on?" I demanded.

"At the door just then - it's Emma."

After that, I'm not quite sure how things progressed. The flat was tidy and orderly and Lucy noticed that I had ironed my clothes for the week ahead. Though I say so myself, I am quite a good chef and I made her an unspectacular but filling dinner and we opened some wine. She seemed a little more subdued than earlier and commented pleasantly on some of the 'Anything can happen in Cardiff' campaign posters that I had framed and hung above the sofa when they were rejected in favour of the 'Bring the minors to Wales' adverts.

I suppose that we were just re-discovering what had kept us together all those years ago. But that is no excuse for the fact that two hours later, I was lying on top of her listening to the sound of moans, grunts and other bodily pleasures while my mind was playing a constant repeat of 'I am screwing a dead woman! Oh God, I'm not using a condom! I could die! I'm screwing a dead woman!'. A loud moan from Lucy brought me back to my senses but I couldn't help but gaze down at her and think 'In ten minutes time, I am going to be lying beside her and this is going to make even less sense.' Lucy grabbed my shoulders and yelled out loud.

Three minutes later, I was lying beside her and it made even less sense. I had just had sex with a dead woman - and she was good. Lucy wrapped her arms around me and I drifted off into troubled dreams.

*   *   *   *   *

The next morning I woke up early to find out that she had gone. A note on the pillow read 'Good morning, sleepy. I've gone to see Phil - I tried to wake you but you were dead to the world.' Have I mentioned yet that death gives people a really bad sense of humour? Night of the Living Dead - don't make me laugh! The Dead are not going to come after you with a chainsaw, they're more likely to knock on your door and strike you down with a painful pun.

There was no answer when I phoned Phil's place. I sat down on our sofa in my dressing-gown and switched on the TV. Our sofa? Yesterday it had been my sofa - yes, it had had a life years ago as 'our sofa' (it was a wedding present) but, no, this current tatty incarnation was known as my sofa. Only now did I see how tatty it really was. I would make it my first task when this nightmare was over to replace it. Nothing made sense any more. I could not bear to think about anything so I watched TV instead.

The Sunday morning TV was as uninspired as it always is. Religious services - oh to be a Roman Catholic at this moment, to turn up at Confession and say 'Forgive me, Father, for I have sinned. I have slept with a dead woman.' I imagined the priest considering carefully before asking, 'Was she dead at the time that you had sex with her?' and I would say, 'No, not at all, Father. She was very much alive.' He would ponder in that way that religious men have and then say, 'In that case it's seven Hail Marys and don't do it again.'

I switched to a news programme on BBC2. Apparently, South Wales had seen several sightings of dead people over the last week. I was a little stunned - in all the fuss of meeting Phil again and then Lucy I had not realised that my experience might not be unique. The usual stories about housefires in Wrexham and award-winning gardens in Powys seemed a little insignificant. I turned up the volume and chewed on my cornflakes.

People were claiming to have met dead relatives - apparently it was not an uncommon phenomenon, there were always one or two each year. However, it was the sheer volume of dead sightings over the last week that had taken the police and local government spokespeople by surprise. Dwr Cymru Welsh Water were investigating claims that a local reservoir had been contaminated with a powerful hallucinogenic while Channel 4 was appealing for any dead people to come on a forthcoming chat show discussion on the theme 'Dead people - the new victims of discrimination?'.

I paced up and down the front room, occasionally glancing at the cars outside in the hope that something would make sense. Ideas raced through my mind, but it was an endurance race, not a sprint. At last Phil answered when I tried the phone. Maybe an hour or two had passed and I was still in my dressing-gown.

"Wow, Tim," he exclaimed, "You never told me Lucy was such fun."

"She's not," I answered.

"We went over to the pub for lunch - there was me, Emma and Lucy sitting at this table and they had both finished their drinks. The barman walks over and, looking at their empty glasses, says 'Are these two dead?' and Lucy answers. 'Yes we are, but we've come back to haunt you.'"

"Are you drunk?" I asked.

"Well, I did have a few. The girls have gone out to meet with some more of their dead friends. Emma's lovely. She's been here a week looking for me you know. She's sweet and is so happy that I moved on from moping about her - she said it wasn't my fault she died ... I think I may even have another chance with her ... I don't know, do you think it's possible to sleep with a dead person?"

"Oh don't be pathetic, Phil. Of course it isn't - what would happen if she got pregnant?" I snapped.

"Oh ... yes, you're right. Be a bastard thing to do. Ah well - Lucy thinks she knows why they're here and Emma's just wondering around amazed that shops are open on Sundays now. This afternoon I'm going to surprise her with the revelation that pubs are open on a Sunday afternoon - and wait till she discovers alcopops!"

I put the phone down. I had an ordered and correct life. I was going somewhere doing a job I enjoyed. There was a stapler, a staple-remover, two black pens, three highlighter pens and a ball of elastic bands in my desk at work. I prayed for

Lucy to come back many times, secure in the knowledge that she never would. Things had a place. Alive people belonged on earth, dead people did not. It was like putting a bookcase in the kitchen. I dragged a bookcase into the kitchen. It seemed to prove to me that the order of things remained unchanged. There were now black marks on the carpet.

I went for a stroll in Bute Park in the afternoon, but I could not shake my anger at having survived the tragedy of my life so well, for not having gone out and found someone else, for not having becoming so uncaringly cheerful as Phil. There was a slight chill in the autumn air and I stopped on a bench by the river and huddled into my coat. How often had I said 'it was what Lucy would have wanted' and never realised that I was wrong?

In the evening, my hand hovered over the phone with my mother's old number in my head ... surely if dead people were appearing then ...? I cried on the sofa. A meal for one and unfunny late night TV comedies were my companions and then I cried in bed until I slept, the hope distant in the back of my mind that maybe next week it would make sense.

*   *   *   *   *

Phil answered my fourth attempt to phone him on Monday morning. It was 8.38 a.m. and Lucy had not returned from visiting him the day before. He sounded bleary and tired and I was determined to be sensible about this.

"Yeah ... yeah," he was saying in a rough voice, "we went back to the pub ... yeah, there was ... oh, I don't remember ... some kind of karaoke and ... err ... hey, we went into the city centre for chips in Caroline St ... ooo, I am phoning in sick today. Thank God I'm self-employed."

"What about the women?" I demanded.

"I didn't lay a finger on them, you bastard. Emma ... she went to bed in the spare room, Lucy's ... she crashed out on the sofa."

I thought about this for a moment, "Where are you sitting, Phil?" I asked.

"On the so ... f ... huh? Hold on ..." There was the sound of unco-ordinated feet, doors opening and a light curse. "Damn, they've gone - to the ... there's a note ... I think it's in Welsh ... no, it's just ... just upside down. It's blurry. How do you write blurry? Ahem. Oh ... she's gone to see you, she wants us all to meet up at The Discovery pub."

I started tidying the home for when she returned. I often did that, looking after our home, making sure that everything was in its proper place. I went to move some magazines off the sofa and then I stopped. Today, just for today, I would leave magazines on the sofa. I would head straight for the pub.

I reached The Discovery and found Lucy sitting in the lounge. It is an odd pub. Cardiff was the last place in Britain that Captain Scott's doomed Antarctic expedition of 1912 stayed in. The Discovery is a pub which has an Antarctic expedition theme. On a cold and raw day, the photographs of iceberg that hung around the bar were hardly very warming.

Lucy was sitting on a seat over in the corner, dressed in dark and comfortable clothes that I imagine she must have buy from a cheap store in the last few days. Unlike Lucy to be so unconcerned about her image, I thought. Two pints of beer sat on the table in front of her.

"Hello." I said.

"Hello," she replied, "I got you a drink."

"Thanks. The other two will probably be a little while."

"Yeah, I know. That was partly the point. I know it's been a shock to you but I think that I have even more of a shocking piece of news to come - and I don't know how much time I've got. So I wanted us to have a proper talk for once."

"Okay. What do you want to know?" I asked, sipping on my pint.

"Is there anything you've wanted to say to me all this time?"

I knew exactly what I wanted to say. I had paced away no end of hours thinking about it and knowing that I never would say it. Not many people get a second chance at anything and when it comes to talking to ex-wives there is very little chance for any kind of sensible discussion.

"Yes. I don't think you'll necessarily like it either. But I couldn't ever say it to you before. You were ill. Everyone loves you when you're ill, you know? People at work who I know never gave a damn about you before used to come up to me for daily updates on your health. Everyone said how awful it must have been for you."

"Well, it was," she said plainly, staring at me over an undrunk pint.

"Yes, I know and everyone knows that. But no-one ever thinks about the people who look after ill people. No-one thinks how hard it is for them. You wake up with pains in the night and I comfort you and you go to sleep. But I stay awake worrying. You can't get to work in the morning so you go back to sleep, I have to go on working. I am constantly worn out from looking after you but all you or anyone else sees is how much you are suffering."

"And so I was. No-one asked you to look after me," she said with some puzzlement.

I took a pause to sip long and slow on my pint. Then I looked up at her, emboldened by the alcohol, the amount I had said already and even the photos of the dead explorers on the icebergs

"There was a time when you were still at home and you were lying on the sofa watching TV. I had been at work - it was another horrible day when I was just exhausted. I came back and started to cook you a meal. It was all going well when I heard you scream. Of course, I ran through as quickly as I could, my tea still in my hand. And do you know what? Do you know what? I cuddled you and asked you what was wrong and all you could do was scream at me because I hadn't put my mug of tea down on a coaster. That was it. And the first scream? The first scream was because you'd dropped the TV remote control. Big panic!"

I sighed heavily after this little speech and took a long drink as she stared across at me. She still had not started drinking.

"I was horrible to you. I know I was ill but you'd be amazed how easy it is to think that that allows you to do or have whatever you want. I'm sorry."

"No, no, it doesn't matter now. You died and with all those crazy bereaved thoughts I realised that I was mourning the you that I knew before you became ill. That was the Lucy I loved not the Lucy that you became. And that's a terrible, frightening thought and maybe that's why I was so desperate to hang on to what you were."

Lucy stared at me for a while and then sipped on her pint. It all reminded me of what Phil said about how trivial the world was. Lucy had worried about having a mug stain on the table when she was facing something far more serious. Out of the corner of my eye, I could see that Phil and Emma had entered the pub and gone to the bar, hand in hand like lovestruck teenagers again, so full of laughter and happiness, forgetting once again the inevitable end of everything.

"I moved a bookcase into the kitchen today and …" I started.

"And I would have killed you if you'd done that when we were married," she mused, "And you're right. I wouldn't do that now. But it's too late for me. It's too late for you too, but you're right. I'm sorry."

Phil and Emma sat down in seats next to us, both chuckling at some private moment. They stopped when they saw our serious faces. Lucy took a long, deep breath and then spoke.

"I firmly believe that tomorrow is the last day that this world will exist. I know that sounds alarmist and crazy but I think that's why we're all appearing here and Emma will confirm that we've been told to go to a point in Cardiff Queen Street at midnight tomorrow night."

Emma nodded, "It used to be the Apocalypse nightclub, I think."

"Would have been a nice irony, Em, but I think it was actually the Zone, Apocalypse was down the road. Shame that. I just think that the four of us should take the opportunity to have some fun before we all go."

Phil and I were staring at the women. This really was crazy. Lucy had only just returned and now she was talking like some millennial-angst driven nutcase. I moved to speak but Phil was there first.

"Penarth?" he said simply. "Why not? It's full of pensioners waiting for the inevitable but if you're going to die, you might as well die somewhere where there's a pier."

"We could have a picnic," added Emma with a smile, "there's a cliff walk and a clearing where on a sunny day you can see up the Bristol channel to the bridge to England. It's the most beautiful spot on earth."

"That's the two bridges now, Em," corrected Lucy.

"This is crazy. This is stupid." I objected. "Why Cardiff? Why not Jerusalem or Los Angeles or Swansea for heaven's sake?"

"You always wanted to put Cardiff on the map," commented Phil, "the Day of Judgement's a pretty good one to host. Unfortunately, the day you put Cardiff on the map is also the day the map is destroyed but any fame is better than no fame."

"This is madness."

Yet before I knew it, I was being whisked out through the hubbub to Phil's car. I mumbled something about needing sunglasses but Phil had all the provisions for a seaside picnic in his car. God, we were going to picnic at the end of the world - how thoroughly depressingly British. I barely spoke as Phil drove through the suburbs towards Penarth Road and a slight glimpse of sunshine behind the clouds. The girls just sat in the back pointing at the occasional new building or closed shop.

"Do you think this is the end of the world?" I burbled to Phil as he took a corner on the way to the sea.

"I don't know," said Phil connecting his phone into the speaker system, "But I do know a great little ice-cream parlour down in Penarth."

And the music started playing - it was a copy of some of Phil's favourite records. He was right - we could all die tomorrow, but what did it matter? Here was now and here was happy.

As he drove us through the genteel calm of the sunshine-soaked seafront of Penarth we both sang along -

"And what they' singin'

Back to back, belly to belly,

I don't give a damn, 'cause I done dead already

Back to back, belly to belly,

At the zombie jamboree."

Meet Jo Bloggs

"I beg your pardon?" said the receptionist politely.

"Jo Bloggs," repeated the young woman with the big backpack squashing her towards the floor.

The receptionist looked confused and slowly stroked a hand through his carefully-flattened hair.

"Joe Bloggs? Well, in that case I'm 'M.Mouse'. We'll need your name, Miss."

The woman looked as though she had made an explanation many times before.

"Jo Bloggs," she repeated, "my mother was Mrs Bloggs and my father was Mr Bloggs. They named me Joanne - or Jo for short. I am sure you understand, Pete."

Peter the Receptionist looked even more baffled for a moment, but then remembered that his badge clearly indicated that he was Peter and that you could ask him for help about anything. He regained his composure.

"And you're staying for one night with us?"

"One night," smiled the woman, "and then I am off for a thousand miles."

"Even the journey of a thousand miles starts with a first step," replied Peter without really thinking.

"What is that, some band lyric?"

"I think so, sorry - could you sign here, please, Miss Bloggs."

"Ms."

Jo moved to sign the register but as she did so, the weight in her backpack shifted to the right and she started to overbalance. She caught herself on the reception desk and steadied back up. A metal mug hanging from her backpack banged against the side of her. She smiled weakly at Peter. She did not look as though she had done this very often. She did not look as though she had done this at all.

"What's 'Ms'?" asked Peter.

Jo righted herself and took a moment to breathe in and regain her balance. It was only here that Peter saw that she had placed a plastic bag down in front of the desk. She had tried to pick it up when she started to overbalance. Jo pushed her glasses up her nose - Peter noticed that they had a makeshift wire around the back of her head to stop them falling off.

This would probably be useful for a hiker. Jo's glasses were of the large and round kind that were fashionable and also inappropriate for a hiker.

"'Ms' is the name that you should call all women as it stops you knowing whether they are married or not."

"That's clever," reflected Peter thoughtfully, "there should be something like that for men."

Jo had regained her balance and she bent down carefully and picked up the plastic bag. She smiled as she did so, as if thinking that this was a great skill for a hiker that she had mastered. She placed the plastic bag on the reception desk.

"Right, show me wear to sign and I'll have my room key."

"Here and here. Have you been to Chepstow before?"

"Okay, here's my autograph ... and no, never been to Chepstow before."

"I can recommend a visit to the castle and why not take a trip over the old bridge to England. You can visit two countries in one trip."

Jo looked at the receptionist as if she was going to straighten up to her full height and ask him if she looked as though she was going to visit the castle, but she was too tired for sarcasm. She also thought that if she straightened up to her full height then she might fall over backwards.

"I'm walking a thousand miles. I am going to find myself."

Pete really wanted to say something along the lines of having woken up and found himself in bed that morning but the reason that he wore a smart waistcoat and tie was because he was paid not to say things like that.

"Oh yes?" was the non-sarcastic reply, made while the computer churned through Jo's details.

"Yes. Wales Coastal Path and then Offa's Dyke. It's a thousand miles in all."

"Is that a thousand miles? Who would have thought that we had such a big country!"

"Oh yes."

"Would you like a hand with your bag?"

"No," replied Jo Bloggs definitely. She did not need help from anyone.

* * * * *

"I am the unluckiest person alive," said Jo Bloggs as the barman filled her wine glass.

"Mmm?" he replied with professional detachment.

"Oh yes, I have had my share of bad luck. You know what happened last month - I had tonsilitis!"

"What's so unlucky about that? Three eighty, by the way."

"What's so unlucky! Here ..."

"Hey, shut your mouth, I don't want to look in there, thank you!"

"No tonsils. No tonsils! N ... O ... tonsils. Taken out when I was a child and then I still get bloody tonsilitis all these years later."

"I didn't know you could get tonsilitis if you didn't have tonsils ..."

"Oh yes, it's caused by the influenza virus so you can still ..."

"I need to serve this guy down the bar."

The barman moved away from Jo and so she went back to rocking her wine glass between her hands. The Lamb & Flag was quiet on a Monday night and the wooden bar stool was not all that comfortable. She surveyed the low-beamed interior of the pub. There were people gathered at some tables in a far corner and a gambling machine blinking an invite to whoever passed, but generally it was a quiet Monday. Jo kept talking even though the barman - Roger, as she would find out later - was serving a man who looked as though he had come to the Lamb & Flag every week for the last forty years.

"I am going to walk a thousand miles and find myself," continued Jo to the near-empty bar, "I'll really get to the bottom of who I am and what I want. Who am I? Where do I belong? I will answer these questions."

"How?"

Roger had returned. He was a quiet-mannered man, short and dark and much more suited to locking up on a quiet Monday night than splitting up a fight on a Saturday night.

"Haven't you read any of those things where people go out into the countryside and find themselves?"

"Yeah, I 'spose - my partner made me watch one of those films over Christmas. Your kind of thing, I guess, woman went off hiking to 'find herself' and all that. You've thrown away your hair straighteners, then?"

"Ah ... well ... I did actually pack them. I know I'm camping, but I thought that maybe ..."

"No kids then?" asked Roger, not usually the man to chat to customers, but feeling generous with his time tonight.

"What?"

"You obviously don't have any kids. I have two little ones now - love 'em to bits of course, but you can't just take off for three or four months. Bills to pay, mouths to feed and all that. Would you like to see pictures of them?"

What was it about proud fathers that they always wanted you to see photos of their children? Oh yes, they really look like they are children was Jo's normal response to those moments. She shook her head instead and shifted a little unsteadily on the bar stool as if the backpack was still pulling her over to the left.

"They're my reason for getting up in the morning," continued Roger, "number one was a bit of a surprise but, you know, you learn as you go along and ... ah, no, what were you saying?"

Jo smiled and took a swig of her wine.

"I was saying that I was going to find myself. You know, my purpose. And no, I don't have children. Odd that, isn't it? At school, having sex was like the radical rebellious thing to do but then there was Jane Cordwell who ended up pregnant and was moved to her aunt's in Caerleon to avoid the shame. Not that the boys were interested in me ..."

Roger laughed and started to wipe down the used glasses behind the bar. "At least you were female. Boys who never got a teenage kiss are ten a penny."

"It's not easier, believe me. But then I was going to say that when you get to the workplace, you are told not to get pregnant as it will ruin your career. Right up until your early 30s and then suddenly it's like ... well, what can I say? If you go on YouTube and your details are female and early 30s then every ad you see will be for pregnancy tests, finding out if you are pregnant, babies, babies, babies ... everything that says YOU SHOULD BE PREGNANT, WHY AREN'T YOU PREGNANT, WHAT IS WRONG WITH YOU!"

The last words were spoken a little too loudly for the bar and some people from the corner table turned around to look. A few more customers were coming in and Roger smiled at them.

"That's never happened to me."

"Of course not, you're a man. That's my point. You get ads for Russian brides and come to Las Vegas where your accent is an aphrodisiac. You get to work out your purpose for yourself."

By now, Roger was serving other customers, but he kept the wine bottle out on the bar as he had a feeling that Jo would want more from it. Jo sipped idly from her glass and sang to herself - 'I would walk five hundred miles, I would walk five hundred more' - and thought 'so I will, so I will'.

"Are you here for the quiz?"

It took a moment for Jo to realise that the cheery man with a toothy grin, a microphone and a clipboard was talking to her.

"The what?"

He handed her a piece of paper with a series of photographs on it. "It's a pound to enter, you can always join one of the regular teams."

"Oh, I ... I'm never lucky in those things. I don't even watch telly much."

"Well, here's a bonus for you. Tell me something you know the answer to and I will slip it into the third round. Join one of the teams over there in the corner and they'll think you're a genius."

"Okay, you know what they say - if you're not living on the edge, you're taking up too much room!"

"It's only a pub quiz ..." said the grinning man, but he took out a pen and stood ready to write on his clipboard.

"Okay then ... yes or no ... is it possible to get tonsilitis if you don't have tonsils?"

The quizmaster smiled and tapped his pen against the clipboard, "Well, it should be 'no' so the answer has to be 'yes'".

Jo opened her mouth wide. The man stared at her and wondered what he was supposed to be looking at. Jo shut her mouth.

"Yes. It is. That's the answer. I did ... I ... okay, I'll chip in a pound."

"You should try Darren's team in the corner there. Four of them and of course Linda is with Colin as well but ... but they could do with someone to help them with tonsilitis questions."

*   *   *   *   *

"So what are you running from?" asked Linda as Jo listened thoughtfully to the questions in round one.

Jo had noticed something of a pattern here. The four blokes clearly spent many of their evenings at pub quizzes and the rest of the time memorising trivia. Knowledge of American basketball teams and their nicknames seemed to be key for membership of the group, along with an unspoken dislike of Ian's team (a different set of blokes on another table, who this week were joined with an oddly-dressed man who they joked was a Martian). Linda's role was to occassionally hold Colin's arm and make comments.

"Here we are in round three. Okay, start you with a classic one. What apart from their names do Glasgow Queen Street station and Cardiff Queen Street station have in common?" asked the quizmaster.

As Jo had not answered, Linda repeated the question.

"What are you running from?"

"I'm not running, I'm hiking."

"Okay, what are you hiking from?"

Linda was older than the rest and had a certain directness that burrowed into people and unnerved them.

"Why must I be hiking from anything? I am trying to find myself."

"I'll repeat the question. Apart from their names, what do Glasgow Queen Street station and Cardiff Queen Street station have in common?"

"Nonsense," said Linda, taking a moment to drink from a half pint glass, "people only set out to find themselves if they have something that makes them question who they are. Is it drink? Was it drugs? A bad relationship? What?"

"I wanted to find myself. I am lost and I need to find direction."

Colin and Darren were staring at each other. Darren had just asked if it was number of platforms and Colin was not sure. They had Mick to contribute but Mick was unsure.

"Drugs, then. Don't blame you, get clean, go for a walk. I went through several bad relationships. I'd like to have just been able to up and walk but had bills to pay and the little one from the first bastard, of course."

"I have had a few bad experiences in love, it's true."

"I think," said Colin finally, "that it's that neither station is actually on a street called Queen Street."

Mick brightened up at this and nodded enthusiastically. They both looked at Darren. As team captain, Darren's decision was final. They trusted him, his intervention over Belgium's progress in the Davis Cup had led them to a one point victory several months before. He also knew all the nicknames of American baseball teams.

"It took me a long time to realise that a lot of the men - like these guys - are actually decent human beings who may be a bit inept, but they'll treat you well and that matters."

"Question two - in which country is the largest glass-domed building in the world?"

Jo was a little uncomfortable but felt that she ought to defend her motivation, "I've had bad break ups. I've got a job in Newport that isn't satisfying, I ..."

"Mother hate you?"

"No! I mean, we have our disagreements, but why do I need to be running from something?"

"We're all running from something."

"One more time - question two - where is the largest glass-domed building in the world?"

The quizzers were contemplating. Mick blew out as if he was still allowed to smoke in pubs and had just taken a long drag on a much-needed cigarette, "We all know it's the National Botanics, but which country does he want?"

"Look at him," replied Darren, "does he look like someone who thinks Carmarthenshire is in Wales or in the UK?"

The quizmaster was standing with his back to the team. Jo was unsure of how you told what he believed about geography just from his looks. Furthermore, Linda was annoying her - she was still speaking.

"It started fine, that was true. He only started getting violent a year or two into it. You start trying to find the way to stop it. Perhaps if I do this, perhaps if I do that ... maybe, just maybe ... maybe today I will find the way to make things different. If anyone should have walked out it should have been bloody me!"

"Why didn't you?"

"Not as easy as you think, young 'un. Then when Bridget came along - well, he had a hold on me then, didn't he?"

Colin overheard a little of this and reached over and gave his girlfriend a showy squeeze and a kiss on the forehead. She smiled coyly.

Jo sat in silence for a while and drank her wine. She had walked back to the bar to ask for a refill when question three started.

"Question three - it's a simple yes or no this time-question three - is it possible for someone without tonsils to get tonsilitis?"

There was a murmur from among the quizzers as they heard a question that was not from the usual quiz books. Jo waved at Roger and pointed at her glass. Hopefully he would refill it while she was making her contribution to the team. She dashed back across the bar. The quizmaster gave a toothy grin as he saw how quickly she was moving. Once she arrived at the table, she found that her team were pretty much in agreement.

"It has to be a 'no'," was Darren's summation.

"No! It's yes!" said Jo dramatically.

They looked at her and pondered her dramatic intervention. Jo opened her mouth and pointed down her throat. They all stared.

"It has to be a comedy question," explained Darren with just a little too much patience, "it has to be. It sounds as though the answer should be 'yes' as that would make it funny. You know, it's like the one 'how long after the first photo was produced was the first pornographic photo produced - one week, one month or one year?' ... the answer has to be a week because that's the funny answer."

"So ...?"

"So," continued Colin, "this guy knows us too well and he must be throwing in a question to trick us. The answer has to be 'no' because he is fooling us into thinking that it is a comedy question when it is not really."

"Yes, but I know that it is 'yes'".

Mick smiled, "Look, I know you're new to the team, but we've been winning this quiz for some months now. We know how this guy works. Trust us on this one - it's a reverse comedy question, it has to be!"

"No, I know the answer!" said Jo insistently, opening her mouth and pointing down her throat again.

"Will you stop doing that!"

"Darren's decision is final," added Colin.

"How are you doing on question three? It's one for all tonsilitis sufferers! Yes or no - can you get tonsilitis if you do not have tonsils? Mine's a pint of the usual Roger - we're coming up to the first break."

"You're not listening to me!" shouted Jo with frustration, "I know the answer!"

Over at the bar, Roger had re-filled her wine glass. It was a pleasant view.

*　*　*　*　*

Jo Bloggs awoke the next day with a slightly tired head. Her team had lost the pub quiz to Ian's team and there had been some recriminations.

Luckily it was by more than one point, so the answer to the 'comedy question' had not been decisive. However, she had taken the opportunity to leave.

She looked over at the other bed in the room. Her backpack was huge. She really had packed everything that she might need and more. The metal mug still hung down from the bottom, the camping equipment was squeezed up one side and a water bottle hung on the other side. The top of the pack bulged with her sleeping bag. She had packed several months of clothes inside ... and books ... and maps ... and a change of shoes. She had a compass and a whistle and a charger for her phone just in case she did find somewhere public in the wilderness. She had a notebook and pens, she had water purification packets, she had ... for the first time since she started this journey of a thousand miles, she looked at her pack and decided that she had packed too much.

Jo realised that what she had really wanted was to take everything with her, to have an adventure without leaving behind what she knew. She wanted the discomfort of adventure with the comfort of home.

Pulling back the sheets, she crossed the short distance to the other bed and tried to haul the backpack on to her shoulders. She swung it around with just a little too much speed and force and she fell straight over backwards on to her bed.

Jo stared at the ceiling. It was one of the patterned kind and you had to admire the skill of whoever had made the neat swirling seashell patterns. Did they do it across the whole ceiling and then put in the light fitting or did they have to work around the light fitting?

Joanne Louise Bloggs sighed. From her position held down by her backpack, she decided that she was a nerdy, whiny overpacker with not very much to complain about. Perhaps instead of walking for the next three months, she ought to go home and get on with the life that she had. She swore under her breath. Day one and just her bloody luck, she had already found herself. There was an irony to that, but it was not a pleasant one.

That was the point when Jo Bloggs decided to go home. Some days life just beats you about the head with the irony stick.

Sometimes the journey of a thousand miles **is** the first step.

Do Not Ask for a Refund

"I had forgotten how crispy potatoes are when they are done in the oven," said John as he pierced a baked potato with a fork.

"I know," said Sally, balancing a plate, a bowl of salad and a small child across only two hands.

"It's such a lovely conservatory you have built on the back here too."

"Mmm," was the reply this time as Sally passed the small child to her mother-in-law, the bowl to her husband and the plate to her brother-in-law. She then realised that her hands were empty and took the plate back.

"Oh, we have never had any truck with this microwave craze," said the mother-in-law, "if you have the time you should do a potato properly. When you've finished with the tuna Sal, pass it over to Timmy."

Sally's husband groaned at hearing his mother's version of his name. It was a battle that he had given up fighting for the moment and his wife gave him an indulgent smile to acknowledge this.

"You've gone back to work then, Sally?" asked John, in between mouthfuls.

"Yes," said Sally, now balancing the small child on her knee while trying to eat some mouthfuls of tuna mayonnaise from her plate, "I have this great job down at ... babe, will you pick up, Ethan?"

Timmy never objected to a diminutive name from his wife and bent down under the table to pick up a crawling child from a sea of Lego.

"Do watch the Lego if you stand up," he cautioned John, though John had already learned to step carefully to avoid the toys.

"You know how often people say 'that's two hours of my life I'll never get back'? Well, you can do, people just don't know about it ..." continued Sally.

"I'd never heard of it," interrupted her mother-in-law, "had you?"

"Never," replied John as the brother-in-law mumbled agreement too.

"It's based in Crewe station – in the same office as where you get refunds for trains being more than eight minutes late."

"Bit of a commute from here?" asked the brother-in-law.

"Three stops on the train and my office is in the actual station."

"More salad?" asked the mother-in-law, offering the bowl with outstretched arms that suggested that John ought to accept whether he wanted any more salad or not.

"Mum! You're interrupting what Sally has to say," said Tim from the far end of the table.

"Oh 'scuse me for being here – where's your Dad gone?"

"He's looking at that back gate. I've kept him a potato in the oven."

"Mark my words Sally, get these two little ones into the habit of eating dinner with their Dad and any others you are going to have."

"Mum!"

"I think that I can stop at two, Fiona."

"I've heard," interrupted John, "that if you have one child then you can keep one eye on the child and one eye on the television. With two children you can keep an eye on each one. Three children and you need arms as well as both eyes all the time."

The parents at the table laughed.

"How many children do you have then, John?"

"None – it's never happened for my girlfriend and me but, you know, we're happy with that. It's great being able to play with other people's children and then hand them back when there is parenting to be done. And they'll say 'oh you don't know what it's like being a parent' but I think that anyone who knows when to hand them back knows exactly what it's like!"

Fiona – John had not been introduced to her by a name other than 'Mum' until a few moments before – laughed and took the salad bowl back from him. Momentarily, John wondered if the test was eating salad until you made a pithy observation. If it was, then he was going to have to eat a lot of salad. He turned back to Sally and asked her to carry on about her job.

"Only part-time, of course, what with these two – if it wasn't for the grandparents we'd been sunk – but yes, it's a really little-known government bureau. It works just like the late train refunds. You have 28 days to fill in a form and you can reclaim time that you think that you will never get back."

"And they can pay you back ... in time?"

"Oh, don't start me on the IT system for repayments!"

There was laughter from the rest of the family and John cut into his potato and picked up some of the salad that had accumulated on his plate. Sally had put her fork down and was now pulling faces at her daughter in the hope of keeping her entertained.

"Their system is so outdated, it's ridiculous," said Tim.

John had seen Tim playing with a large bank of computers in one room of the house and guessed that he was some kind of IT engineer.

"It's crazy. You know, typical public sector, they were running a version 8 system and then bought in this version 9 system but without replacing the 8. So, they're running two systems simultaneously. It wouldn't happen in business ..."

Tim stopped when he realised that Sally was staring at him. She handed him their daughter.

"She's not settling – I'll grab Ethan and get him sorted, you take this one."

Fiona the Mother-in-Law waved at Ethan as he was carried past her and soon Sally was somewhere else in the house and the four of them were left sitting out in the conservatory, stars and streetlights now shining in from outside. For a while, three of them ate in a contented silence.

"I can't believe he's still out there working on that damn gate," muttered Fiona, but no-one responded.

"It's very good. That place Sally works. I did a claim last year," said the brother-in-law to continue the conversation.

"Oh yeah? What happened?" asked John.

"Well, it was like this. I was seeing some old film – I don't know, Basic Instinct or something like that – and I thought 'woah, there's two hours of my life that I'll never get back'. You know, like you say. You do something and then it is really boring and you say it and ..."

"You're labouring the point, darling," said his mother gently, placing a quietening hand on his arm.

"Oh right. Anyway, Sal's department looks after the claims."

"I don't get how it works ..." said John.

"Why don't you go and find Dad, Timmy? Simon, you need to eat up. Don't mind them, it's always a bit hectic around here, John."

*   *   *   *   *

The leaves had fallen by this stage of the autumn and a reddish brown path lay beneath Sally and John's feet as they stood in the park together. Simon was somewhere in the playground with the two children, but Sally and John stood by the fence musing on the time that they worked together and the changes in their lives since.

"I still don't understand about your job," said John, "how does it work?"

"Well," said Sally, as though she had had to explain this too often, "you know when you do something boring and say 'that's two hours of my life I am never going to get back'? Well, that is not actually true. You can. It's a compensation scheme, like when your train is late and you lose eight minutes of your day due to engineering work. It's a clever scheme."

"And you pay people ..."

"No, we add time back on to their life."

"That makes no sense."

Sally smiled and motioned for him to follow her into the playground.

"Everyone says that, that's why they don't apply. It's like those bank compensation schemes that people never bother to check out. The refunds office is in the station in Crewe because it got merged with the train delays stuff some years ago. You know, efficiency drives and all that although, of course, we never talk to the train refunds people, whole different area of work. Simon!"

Simon looked up from pushing the swings and waved at them. Sally motioned for him to bring the children back over and he carefully stopped the swings. One of them he would carry, the other would hold his hand.

"It doesn't really work out financially, the job," said Sally, watching the children carefully.

"I'll bet it doesn't – employing people to deal with the cost of adding time to people's lives ..."

"No, I mean with the children. Tim reckons that with the cuts to free childcare and everything that we would be better off with me not working, but I like having something to do. Love these two to bits but need a break occasionally. Sorry about the house by the way, we did mean to tidy up."

"Oh, it's nothing, most of my friends have children now, so I am used to it," replied John with a smile.

Sally looked away from Simon's slow progress across the playground and turned to speak to John directly. Rather self-consciously she straightened her woolly hat with a glove.

"The thing is that you do try but they are just so creative with it. Ethan found all Milly's shoes the other day and lined them up with toys in them. When I asked him what he was doing, he said that they were racing cars. Now he thinks that the wardrobe is a garage! Okay, Si?"

"Sure, no problems – think they're getting a bit tired now, though?"

Sally took Milly from her brother-in-law and held her in an arm. Ethan let go of his uncle's hand and ran over to grab his mother's leg.

"Not quite how you remember me on wild nights out in Birmingham ten years ago, eh?" she said to John.

"I don't get this thing about the job still – do you add to people's days?"

"No, no, no – end of life. That's part of the problem – you know how sometimes there are old people who seem to have lived past a healthy point to ... well, you know ... we are starting to wonder if that is because we have given them a ... ooo, Millicent Milly Moo? You're a struggler today, aren't you? You tired? Shall we get you and your brother home?"

They walked up the leafy path to the road, the chill of the evening starting to settle in over the passing warmth of the afternoon. They were all wrapped up against the cold but walked as briskly as they could – at least, the adults walked briskly, the children dawdled as if there were no end to the day.

At the traffic lights on the main road, Sally lifted her son up and told him to push the button and 'wait for the green woman'.

"The green woman?" asked John.

"No reason it could not be a woman. She could be wearing trousers, it's only a silhouette. Start on equality from the beginning, it's the only way."

John smiled to himself because he knew that from that day onwards he would stand at traffic lights waiting for the green woman to tell him that it was safe to cross.

*   *   *   *   *

John sat in the passenger seat with his overnight bag balanced awkwardly on the floor between his feet. The car smelt slightly of petrol and rattled when it accelerated, but when Sally's father-in-law offered him a lift to the nearest mainline station, he felt that it would have been rude to refuse.

So far the conversation had only been about the weather, travel and potholes, the last of these being caused by a sign that read 'Cheshire County Council : Combating Potholes' and the comment 'I don't want them to combat them, I want them to fill the bloody things in!'. It was polite small talk between John and a man who he had only heard referred to as 'Dad' for the weekend.

"I don't like to comment really," said the older man, "but I don't like this job that she's doing."

There was an awkward silence, as if the older person in the car had said something racist and John was struggling with whether he should tell him off for this.

"Oh, that's an interesting comment," was John's considered answer. It was not agreement, it was not criticism, generally speaking it was generally speaking.

"Look, I don't mind women working. I'm all for it if someone is there to take care of the children. You know, I'm not old-fashioned. But this job – you do know that it is terrible discrimination, don't you?"

"Discrimination?" said John, puzzled even more now.

"Discrimination! Who is going to have the time and money to claim back lost hours? Rich people that is who, not your every day worker like I was. Didn't exist when I was your age, of course, but I was too busy trying to provide for Fiona and the kids to worry about hours lost to bad movies or dull work meetings."

"Surely the rich live longer than the poor anyway?"

"And this just makes it worse. Look at the Royal Family – they almost always live over 90 that lot. And why?"

"They have an undemanding lifestyle, great comfort and the attention of the best medical opinions in the world?"

"I reckon that they send out one of the flunkies to claim time back for them all the time. Royal Variety Performance? Bet they're rubbing their cosily-gloved hands together thinking 'ooo, that's another four hours to claim back'. The poor idiot sitting on the sofa watching it just gets up the next day and has to get on with it. That's discrimination."

There was a silence as the Dad-in-law manoeuvred the car around a roundabout without indicating properly.

"Do you actually believe it though? It seems ridiculous to me!"

"Of course, I believe it. It makes sense. You can get a refund when you waste time because your train is late, why not for other things? I just think that it's like so much else in the world, you know that it's the poor who pay and furthermore ..."

John switched off at this point and stared out the window at the passing houses. Four 'ah-ha's and a 'really?' later, they were at the main station and John was getting out and thanking the older man for his kindness.

*   *   *   *   *

The train rattled into his local station several hours later. There on the station platform, in a woolly hat and the comfy gloves that he bought her last Christmas, was John's girlfriend. The sight of Lizzie's smiling face under the woolly cover lifted his heart. He rushed forward to cuddle her.

"I like it when you're delayed by engineering works," she joked, "it always makes you that much happier to see me."

John kissed her full on the lips. "They said a broken rail somewhere had everything running an hour behind."

"Well," said Lizzie, grabbing his cold hand in her cosy hand, "we'll get you home and warm you up. It's been an extra hour standing out here waiting for you, mind."

"Yeah, I know, that's an hour of your life you'll never ... yeah, there's something I need to talk to you about."

This page has been left intentionally blank

(except of course it isn't)

The Matrix Revisited

[The following bears no resemblance to the classic sci-fi film 'The Matrix', which contains an iconic scene where the main character Neo meets a mysterious man named Morpheus who offers him a choice, a choice that depends on whether he takes a blue pill or a red pill].

Morpheus looked at Neo seriously. He held out his hands and in each one, Neo saw a coloured pill.

"This is your last chance. After this, there is no turning back. You take the blue pill - the story ends, you wake up in your bed and believe whatever you want to believe. You take the red pill - you stay in Wonderland and I show you how deep the rabbit-hole goes," said Morpheus solemnly.

Neo looked back from one hand to the other, a sense of drama building in him. Until recently he had only been Thomas Anderson, computer programmer but now he was hearing the most amazing things about something called 'the matrix'.

"Well ...?" said Morpheus impatiently.

"Ah you see, now, it's a tough decision."

Morpheus stared at Neo intently. "Take the red pill and you ..."

"Yes, I know, I heard you. Hmm ... you started with the red pill this time, is this some kind of

Derren Brown trick where you persuade me to take the pill you want?"

"No," said Morpheus a little testily, "No Neo, this is no trick. You can take either pill, things will happen as a result of your choice. You said that you didn't believe in fate, this is your choice."

Neo looked at Morpheus's outstretched arms a little longer and scratched his chin.

"It's a tough one Morph, you see, there was this night out in Swansea when my mate Gareth offered me a blue pill. I thought that I could see these weird colours and shapes and all sorts of chaos - screaming, shouting, people falling in and out of doorways and over in the street."

"This is not that kind of pill, Neo."

"Oh no, that was before I took the pill, that was just Swansea on a Saturday night. No, when I took the blue pill, that is when the serious shit started."

Morpheus looked as though his arms were now becoming tired. He looked at Neo carefully and talked with a certain urgency to his voice.

"Neo, if you take the red pill, you may find that Swansea is not real."

"Woah, hold on, you need to be not talking like that. Port Talbot sure, we know that's a figment, but if you are saying that Wind Street on a Saturday night is not real then you and I will have a problem here, we will."

"Neo, I can't explain any more until you make a choice. I thought that you said that you wanted to be in control of your fate."

"I do," said Neo carefully, "it's just that this is a big choice. You keep telling me that this is the most important decision that I can make. I want to get it right. You know, I flunked my GCSE Geography because I made the wrong choice."

"Your GCSE Geography exam was not real."

"You're telling me it was unreal. Bloody knolls I revised but it was all hanging valleys ... can one of these pills reverse my D grade?"

Morpheus put the pills back in his pocket as his arms were starting to become tired and he had spent too long trying to explain things. He stood up and walked around while Neo thought.

"Can you go back over which pill is which?"

Morpheus sighed. "Okay, okay, blue pill is back to bed ..."

"Back to reality?"

"Ah-ha yes, if you like. Red pill is about staying in Wonderland, rabbit-hole, white rabbit and all that kind of stuff."

"Hmm ... the white rabbit. There's a statue of him in Llandudno, you know. That's why I followed it, I thought it was some kind of seaside free offer."

"Neo!" shouted Morpheus more angrily now, "It is not about Llandudno! Llandudno is not real! Listen to me! You have been chosen, we need you!"

"You're getting awfully close to me there, fella. Thank you, now back off ... what was the choice again?"

Morpheus sighed and sat back down. He tried to calm down and once again open his hands to show Neo the two pills. Others had been chosen, but this was the first time any one of them had refused to make a choice.

"You have to make a choice, Neo."

"Why?"

"Don't you see that doing nothing is a choice too. Choosing to go about your life as normal and pretend that nothing is wrong, that is a choice too?"

"What if I went about my life and did nothing but every now and then I thought that there was something more that I was missing - like my mate Garry with his Tarot cards. Why do I have to choose? You come in here with your pills saying oh yes, you can be this or be that - why can I not choose a bit of both? Isn't that what everyone does? And anyway, how do I know what you are offering in this red pill club of yours? I feel as though I am lined up outside to go in and you are not even telling me if there are any free drinks offers or two for one on vodka shots."

"Okay, Neo, you are the one after all. Let me give you an overview of the other world, the red pill world. It is a world where everything will be explained. It is a world that some ... err ... people would rather that we did not see and so we have to fight them. We need strong minds like yours to help in this fight. We have a small army, but we need you too. There are women who wear shiny black PVC ..."

Neo had grabbed and swallowed the red pill before he had finished the sentence.

"Next time lead with the women in PVC mate," he said as the world around him dissolved.

The Book Had Other Plans

"And then he only goes and says ... are you listening, Darren?"

"What? Oh yes ... look, we'll get seated, here comes the waiter."

The waiter gave a professional smile and took two menus for the customers in front of him. "Table for two, Sir?"

"Three, please," said Darren assertively.

The waiter looked behind the two of them at the empty space in the doorway. He concealed a shrug and led his diners to a table by the corridor to the toilets.

"Welcome to the Piccolo Mondo. Your menus. Will your friend be joining you before the meal?"

He pulled out a chair for Darren's sister to sit in and then placed the menus on the table between them.

"No, we'll be keeping the third seat free," replied Darren.

The waiter raised an eyebrow but did not let it stop his speech. "Tonight's specials are on the board, I will bring you some water and some olives while you decide."

When the water arrived, Darren filled a glass for his sister and one for himself. He turned towards the empty chair. "Dad," he said.

"Dad," repeated his sister and raised her glass as well.

It was at this point that Darren removed The Book from his backpack. He was trying to avoid putting the backpack on the empty chair, but there was no room at his feet without emptying it.

"Darren ...? You need to stop reading that book, you're not doing yourself any favours. I read one of the stories in the flat last night, it was nonsense. You've always had your head in the clouds ..."

Darren moved The Book to the adjoining table, in front of the empty seat. He almost thought about opening it for Dad to read, but then decided against it.

"Darren ...? Where was I? There I was standing in the street when a man comes up to me and says 'I love your hair colour'."

"What have you gone this time - it looks pink and blue but ...?" said the brother, staring at his sister's hairs as she twisted a few colourful strands in her hand.

"He asks for a photo. Well, I'm like woah, maybe he is a fashion designer, maybe some kind of big shot. This was back in Cardiff so maybe he is one of those sci-fi shows they film down in the Bay. You know, perhaps I had a gig as Alien #3 ..."

"Mmm?"

"Exactly. So he takes the photo - not a selfie, but a close up shot of the hair. He says - 'I am going to take this down to B&Q for their 'paint match' service, this is just the colour I need for the third bedroom! Can you imagine? He's only interested in the frigging colour for a wall! Not for hair, a wall!"

Darren had emptied all of his backpack at this point and now he could fit it by his feet. The Book fell off the table and on to the empty chair beneath it. It would be hidden when Darren came to pack up one hour and forty-seven minutes later.

"Isn't that Tony from Guildford who works in your office?" asked Darren's sister.

"It is, I think. Who'd've thought it, it's a small world the Piccolo Mondo."

*   *   *   *   *

The Book had enjoyed being with Darren. They took the train together to London every day and Darren was always careful with The Book, even though they were jostled and pushed together in the cramped carriages. It had been while reading The Book that Darren had decided to change his career. Some ignorant commuter wearing too little deoderant had knocked The Book out of Darren's hand while struggling to get out of the train at one of those many suburban stations beginning with 'W'. Darren had reached down to pick The Book up of course (and sworn softly under his breath) but it was at that moment that he also realised how much he hated the 5.20. He took out his phone and searched for some recruitment sites. It was a bold move but it was also the move that The Book knew meant that their time together was coming to an end.

Sophia was The Book's next person. She picked up The Book from the empty seat in the restaurant and asked the waiter if he had an address for the two people who had been there. The man was the waiter, The Book never needed to know the names of anyone else. Whatever his name was, he did not know the two of them. They had not booked in advance and they were not big tippers. He remembered the man talking about his new job and his change of career, it had made him hope that a big tip was on the way to celebrate but no, there was no big tip.

Sophia scowled at him and put The Book by the side of the counter in case they came back. They never came back and she took The Book home with her that night.

* * * * *

It is a few months later and Sophia is making mistakes with her orders. She moves The Book out of the way from where she was reading it in the kitchen, before the resturant opened for the night.

"I don't know why you read that rubbish," said the chef, idly preparing more pasta.

"It's interesting, I found it when ..."

"Yeah, yeah, we know, we know," replied the chef, taking a swift drink from a bottle of water sitting by the ovens, "but I had a look at it, it's nothing to do with the title or the cover. It's rubbish - concentrate on your job and not on entertainment. Let's try to get table four right this time."

"Sure."

Unfortunately, Sophia did not manage to take table four the correct order and the Chef's Special had to be recooked and given for free. It was only a couple of days later that Sophia found herself in the boss's office. The Book was in her bag. The boss was not happy and could give Sophia quite a list of her recent errors. He was a kind man though and he gave her a chance to explain herself.

Sophia started to cry. This unnerved the boss, but he offered her a tissue and asked if anything was wrong. He was expecting some complaint of pressure from someone doing a class in College in her down time or perhaps a difficult boyfriend. However, when Sophia explained that her mother had been diagnosed with a serious heart condition and needed emergency surgery, the boss was lost for words. Sophia had been estranged from her mother for five years now and she only knew this from one of her sisters. She needed to be in St Albans, quite the other side of London.

The boss told her to take as long as she needed and that her job would be waiting for her on her return. Now it was Sophia's turn to be surprised. She had not imagined that an employer would be so understanding. She thanked him, she thanked him too much really, clutched her bag to her side and marched off back to the station.

The Book had enjoyed being with Sophia, but The Book had no intention of going to St Albans. The Book had other plans. Sophia had made a resolution to make amends with her mother and return to her family. The Book was moving on too. There was no more sitting on the bus going to College or going to the restaurant.

* * * * *

Martha picked up The Book from the empty seat on the train. She looked around the carriage and wondered if she could find the person who had left it there. The carriage was deserted now, so she thought that she would take it to lost property. The trouble was that it was a quick turnaround for the train to head out to Swansea. Someone would surely know that and claim the book if it was special to them. There was no dedication in the front, no 'darling Amanda, to celebrate thirty years of love and passion' and so Martha thought probably not. She put it on the trolley and continued to place reservation markers on the back of the train seats.

It was forty-seven minutes later that the ticket collector asked her "What's that book you've got then?"

They were standing in the corridor between coaches E and F. The train had been so crowded on leaving Paddington that Martha had left the trolley between carriages and the ticket collector had not been able to progress far. They had both nodded at the phrase 'leave it until after Reading' and now Martha was reading at Reading.

"I thought you liked those e-book things anyway, romances and what not on the Kindle," added the ticket inspector.

Martha shrugged. "I do," she said, "but I found this one on the train. Thought I could give it in but it's not all bad."

"What's it all about then? Is it another romance thing?"

"It's short stories. It's good if you don't like concentrating for long."

"Oh. How are the kids?"

"Still at home," said Martha with a smile and a laugh, "bought Jordan a bloody suitcase for his 18th but he is still there."

They both laughed. The ticket inspector had been a friend of Martha's from before the divorce.

"You need to tell him to get off his arse and get to College at least. Part-time job somewhere too - don't care where, he can peel potatoes at his age - and study. You don't get nowhere now without an education."

"You know, I've been thinking that I ought to go to College."

The ticket inspector looked down and scratched the back of his neck. He was trying to think of a tactful way of saying something. His conclusion was, "but you're in your thirties."

"Ha!" said Martha and hit him with The Book, "Fifties soon, you bloody charmer. No, I'm serious, why not? Why shouldn't I study? Find out more about the world."

"You've got a job, what's the point?"

"I don't know, it's just ... you know ... you think it's weird for me to be sitting here reading a book? Why? Sure, I haven't read anything serious in a long while but ... why not?"

"Maybe I can read it when you're done and it'll inspire me, unless it's all '50 Shades of Grey'?"

"Definitely not."

"Definitely not read it or definitely not '50 Shades'?"

"'Scuse me mate, when are we getting to Swindon?"

That was the sound of a traveller disturbing them and it meant time for the ticket inspector to check and sell tickets and time for Martha to put the book into the trolley and go and sell coffee and mini cheddars to people stressed from a day out in London.

The Book was only travelling with Martha briefly. In fact, Martha would part company with The Book and not remember that she had not finished it until some years later.

* * * * *

Andrew Williams thought that he had had a true stroke of luck when he picked up The Book from where it had fallen out of Martha's trolley. It was a stupid thing to think, but he needed a book for when he met his girlfriend the next day. Of the two of them, she was the big reader and he wanted to impress her with what he was reading. She would doubtless have found some new work of classic literature to enthuse about and he would have to nod and think how pretty her eyes were. It is hard for a man who is over six feet tall to feel dwarfed by a woman, but his five feet two inches girlfriend had just that effect on him. When she invited him to a book shop, he was slightly thrown and when she explained that it was a book signing by a famous modern author, well, all he knew was that he ought to have a copy of the man's book to sign.

Andrew had enthusiasm and Andrew had love, but he did not have motivation. Monday's worrying became Tuesday's concern and Tuesday's concern became Wednesday's mild panic. Wednesday's mild panic became Thursday's inability to think straight and Thursday's inability to think straight became Friday's preference for putting difficult things to the back of his mind. All the shops had shut for Friday night now and Andrew was on the train wishing that he had thought about how to find a book before Saturday morning. He had none in his house, other than histories of the FA Cup and a book about trains his father had given him.

He fully expected his girlfriend to inform him the next day that commemorations of the Easter Rising of 1916 in Dublin were incorrectly timed since in 1916 Ireland had operated on a different time zone to the rest of the UK. It was the sort of random thing that she knew and he loved her for it, but he at least wanted to have a book for the book signing.

Andrew picked up The Book with such thanks. At first he had thought that he ought to offer it to the woman whose trolley it had fallen from. Andrew was not a thief by nature but sometimes love makes us the worst possible person that we could be (sometimes we call this going to extraordinary lengths for love, when we are trying to be romantic about things like stealing a book that someone has dropped).

When Andrew left the train, his girlfriend was waiting on the platform for him and enveloped him in the kind of hug that says 'I missed you' in the most warm and comforting way. Andrew was no longer panicking though, Andrew had a plan. The Book had a plan, of course.

Everything was glorious from that moment on. Andrew and his girlfriend made up for lost time in every way possible and they were still in bed and giggling like mad teenagers when they realised that the book signing would soon be starting. They laughed as they ran around the flat trying to find the clothes that they had discarded so hastily the night before. The shower was running and they both jumped under the water, pausing only for Andrew to place some soap suds on his girlfriend's nose and then blow the bubble away.

These were things that Andrew felt confident about.

They headed out to the High Street hand in hand. Their footfall on the hill down into town was a little unsteady as they were both moving a little too fast. Andrew swung a plastic bag with his free hand and in it was The Book.

"I can't believe that he is really here. This city. Our city!"

Andrew smiled back and swung her hand even harder. They were a couple made of smiles and giggles that morning.

The bookshop was only down the hill, past the hotel, over the main road and two streets past the Indoor Market. They had been to a poetry reading there before and they often stopped in for coffee in the café. Now the shop had 'Book Signing Today' on a chalk board outside and there was a small queue of people jostling to see the famous author inside.

"It really is him," said Andrew's girlfriend with the nerves of a teenager who has seen a favourite rock star. She squeezed Andrew's hand excitedly.

They queued solemnly. It almost seemed wrong if people had spoken at that moment. The shop was a mixture of the normal retail sounds of a Saturday mixed with the excited hum of people holding books to be signed. They might also have thought of a question for the author to answer.

Andrew's girlfriend went before him. He did not hear what she said but she smiled and nodded at the author as she talked to him. When he had signed her book, she gave Andrew a wink as she moved away.

Andrew presented the author with The Book.

"What is this?" he asked.

"It's err ...," Andrew was lost for words in front of someone he did not know, "I got this book, it's ..."

"Cheese Market of the Future, what the hell does that mean?"

"I don't know, I thought it was ..."

"I wouldn't write anything like that. What is it? Economics or some dull crap? Do you have one of my books to sign?"

"No, I ..."

"Well, ten ninety nine for one from the pile and I will sign it too."

Andrew looked round and he could see his girlfriend watching him, probably thinking that he was asking some great question about where the author found his inspiration. He tried to hand over the money without his girlfriend seeing what he was doing.

The author whistled through his teeth. "The stuff I have to put up with! Here's your autographed copy, have a nice day."

Andrew started to walk away and head towards his partner. He felt relieved. It was like an ordeal finally over.

"Oy you! Tall guy!" came the shout of a famous voice, "you forgot your cheese book!"

Andrew ignored the shouts and soon the next person in line had taken his place and The Book was discarded to one side, almost signed by the wrong author.

Andrew and his girlfriend left to discuss what the great man had said and how lucky Andrew had been to have so long with him. In fact, later that night Andrew would ask his girlfriend what she thought about them looking for a flat together. She would hug him and squeal with delight. Meanwhile, The Book would aim to be in a safe and warm shelf, snuggled up with other books before the night was over.

That was not the end of The Book's journey. The Book's plan had not been to go to that author on that day, The Book had intended to be found by Andrew but then passed on to his girlfriend. From the safety of the bookshelf, The Book would recalculate. It might even have to nip into e-book form to make its next journey.

The next time someone picks up something called 'Cheese Market of the Future', they are not borrowing The Book, The Book is borrowing them.

If You Liked It, You Should Have Put A Flake In It

THE PAST

Steven Tyler sat in a badly-lit seating area of the bar. Badly-lit was just how it should be, he told himself. A white label on his second-best shirt showed that he was 'Steve' – friendly and approachable, he thought. His nerves were calmed slightly by the presence of two young women at the table next to him. They looked attractive, intelligent and worth spending a little time with in conversation.

The woman who was organising the evening walked over to them. Her badge said 'Amanda' and she was clearly still in University, running these nights as an extra way of earning money. What did she know about life, thought Steven. He observed that she knew how to approach young women who did not yet have a label.

"Are you here for the speed-dating?" she asked them with a bright, re-assuring smile.

There was a snort of derision from one of the young women and she replied, "Do we look that desperate?" before laughing.

Steven reminded himself not to get too close to the label-less ones, they were a different tribe and they did not understand the ways of the labelled.

Speed dating is the triage of the dating world. It enables you to quickly sort out the people you meet without spending too much time with them. For the optimist, it condenses the intrigue and excitement of twelve dates into one evening. For the pessimist, it replaces the chance for one person to reject you with the opportunity for twelve people to reject you. Every rational person knows that we are not such shallow people that we can make a judgement about someone in three minutes ... but we do.

Everyone going to a speed dating event needs their 'killer question'. This is not 'if you were going to be a serial killer, what kind of serial killer would you be?' but a question to ask that goes beyond the usual 'who are you, what do you do, where do you live' awkward social small talk. Steven's was ice cream.

Steven had done this once before. It had not been a success. Dates could be divided into a number of categories – those you fancied but who didn't fancy you, those who fancied you but who you didn't fancy, those you had a great time with but there was no spark of attraction there and those who really did not belong in speed dating. One of this last category spent three minutes telling him about how her ex-husband left her 'on Christmas Day for a younger woman'. This phrase was repeated so often that Steven wanted to ask her if she would have been okay if the man had left her for an older woman on Boxing Day. Her favourite ice cream was vanilla which meant that she was dependable and predictable (but possibly repressing a strawberry-loving tendency).

"Your choice of ice cream means something," Steven had to explain to 'Sam I Am' (as her badge said).

"Give me examples," she asked with curiosity.

"Well, raspberry ripple means that you like to mix it up a bit. Tutti Frutti is for people who try to order in Italian in restaurants, especially Chinese restaurants. Any flavour of Magnum means that you only ever buy ice cream in the supermarket."

"What if I don't like ice cream?"

Steven made a note from triage that this woman was beyond saving.

Steven was at heart an optimist. He believed in love and, after the age of 21, you have to be an optimist to believe in love. Each three minutes was a chance to look for that connection that might last a lifetime. On the second night there was a woman from Porthcawl who talked about flood defences, the organiser of an arts film festival who had no interest in Steven's office job, a wonderfully bubbly teaching assistant who had a lot of conversation but no spark and an accountant who said that there were no jokes about accountancy. The ice cream test results were banana (I have more hope than experience - everyone knows that you cannot artificially create the taste of banana), apple crumble (I eat my ice cream somewhere very expensive) and a mixture of strawberry, chocolate and mint choc chip with a flake, sprinkles and some sauce (I annoy people who stand behind me in queues for ice cream).

Then, of course, there was Laura, the midwife from the Rhondda.

THE PRESENT

"So why did you agree to meet me again?" asked Steven.

Laura laughed, "Well, you've already told me that you liked my choice of ice cream."

Steven smiled and clinked his wine glass against hers, "It tells you everything that you need to know."

"Tell me some others that you've met then."

"Well, any ice cream from a small pot means I last ate ice cream in the cinema and I probably have not been to a cinema in a while either. Pineapple is for truth or dare players - you want to challenge them to actually make it taste like a pineapple, though you think that it is probably impossible."

"What if I like ice lollies?"

"Then you are into the divide between lickers and biters."

"What if I like to do both?" asked Laura with a flirtatious smile.

"Hmm ... err ... well ..you never did tell me why you went speed dating."

Laura took a long drink of the fizzy wine and then took a more serious approach.

"I suppose that a few years ago I learnt that everything we have – everything is so very fragile. Yes, I was on my own and all that, ex-had left me yadda yadda yadda, I could tell you all about that but never on a first date ... well ... I was involved in a car accident."

"Oh," said Steven, not really sure what was the best thing to say.

"I was driving along the A48, just at that bit where it narrows to one lane after Culverhouse Cross. Some idiot came speeding past me, way too fast and as I tried to get out of his way, the car spun and I got hit and knocked off the road."

"Woah. That's awful. You didn't hit the speeder?"

"Oh no, he had a fine old day getting to wherever he was going very fast. Probably still tells people that he always chooses the appropriate speed for the road conditions, you know."

"Sure, I know the type. But what about you though, were you okay?"

"Shaken up, but damaged my wrist – arm out trying to cushion the impact," here Laura demonstrated the action rather needlessly across the table, "ended up with a pain that wouldn't go away. Months of physio, had to stop working ... absolute nightmare. One minute driving along with a life that's fine, the next everything changed."

"Woah," said Steven, leaning back and taking a sip of his wine, "That sounds awful. That sounds ... hold on, why does that make you do speed dating? Is it because the whole experience is a car crash? Is it speed that is wrong?"

Laura laughed as she realised that she had really not made much sense with her anecdote. She was distracted momentarily by what she thought was their food approaching, but the waiter carried it to another table. She turned back frustrated and then focused on answering the question.

"No, I mean it made me think about how you have to take a chance in life before it's too late."

"You are refreshingly honest, I like that."

They sat there for a moment in a comfortable, hungry silence. Others might have mistaken it for boredom, but they had a quiet fascination for one another. He liked that she had been distracted by food, she liked that she had felt able to tell him about the accident (and he had listened). Their starter course arrived with them still smiling at each other.

"So," she said, picking up a soup spoon and pointing it at him, "tell me more about this ice cream thing. What others responses have you had from speed dating?"

Steven smiled as she carefully leaned forward trying to balance herself so that her hair did not fall in her soup. She was busy cursing herself for wearing it down or for ordering soup or both.

"It's like this, you can tell a lot about someone by their favourite ice cream."

"Cornetto eaters are demanding, surely. Just one Cornetto, give it to me - no, you can buy your bloody own, you know?"

"Mr Whippy is either for kinky people or people who like titles. No, not Whippy, that's **Mr** Whippy to you!"

"Rum and raisin is for alcoholics, rum 'n' raisin is for alcoholics who cannot spell."

"You're good at this," said Steven with a satisfied smile, "and to think one woman told me that it was sexist."

"It probably is, but I'll bet she ate Weight Watchers ice cream. That says 'I do not understand the point of ice cream'."

They both laughed and Steven stabbed his whitebait starter awkwardly with a fork.

"And what about me," said Laura, throwing her hair back, relieved to be sitting back from the soup, "my favourite is rum 'n' raisin."

"You were wrong about that one. That, of course, is the model of perfection."

THE FUTURE

Steven stretched out on the sofa towards Laura, but she was standing up even before their favourite TV show had finished. Steven made a drama out of grabbing the thin air and then falling where she had been. He felt her warmth on the fabric next to him.

Laura was already in the kitchen and she emerged – after the sound of the freezer opening – with a tub of ice cream and two spoons.

"I started defrosting during the last commercial break."

"You or the ice cream?"

"Cheeky!" exclaimed Laura and punched him playfully on the arm as she sat down again.

Carefully, she removed the lid of the ice cream tub and took a scoop on to her spoon. She motioned it vaguely towards him and then at the last moment pulled the spoon back to her own mouth with a giggle. Before she could swallow, Steven leaned forwards and kissed her full on the lips.

"Mmm, cold but nice!" he said, "Rum 'n' raisin?"

"You can tell a lot about someone from their favourite flavour of ice cream."

There is No Alternative

"Can I borrow a sleeping bag?"

The woman who interrupts what you are doing is dishevelled. She is probably in her 30s but looks older. There is a slightly wild look in her eyes. She asks you again insistently.

"I need a sleeping bag. Not to buy, just to borrow. Please."

You are not sure what to say. She looks at you so earnestly that you feel as though there would be a story behind the request, but would you take the risk?

"Can I borrow a sleeping bag?"

*   *   *   *   *

The café is always the same - the tables, the fold-down seats, the broken sliding door under the staircase that is marked for staff only ... Sometimes there are Christmas decorations, sometimes there are not, but Laura recognises the café every time that she is here. It is the one constant in her life – that and needing a sleeping bag.

"Have you ever heard about the theory of alternative universes?"

She looks a little tidier now. You are sitting across the table from her and she self-consciously brushes her hair back. Her face still has that hint of wildness to it, but the mug of tea that you bought her seems to be helping. You came to Llanidloes for a hot drink to break up the drive between camp sites. You are cautious and so you ask her what she means.

"Alternative universes – every time we make a decision, we create a new universe. One in which we chose one course of action, the other is where we chose the other course of action. We stay in the one universe of course, but there are thousands, millions, countless really, others that have been created by our other choices."

"Why do you need a sleeping bag?" you ask politely.

"A long while ago I found out that I could go between these universes – there are a few people who can. This café is the only link between them."

You look around the café and stare at the non-descript decor, newspapers and early morning breakfasts. There is a mother and son sharing a fry-up, a group of older people talking over tea, three waitresses chatting about where they are going that night ... it is hard to believe that this might be the centre of the universe.

"You are thinking that it is hard to believe that this might be the centre of the universe."

You manage a motion somewhere between shaking your head and nodding. You let her continue.

"I know, I know, it should be London or Los Angeles or New York but it is not, it is a café in Llanidloes. I come in from one universe but if I concentrate hard enough, I can go out into another."

"Do it then," you challenge her cheekily.

"No, I am tired of it now, I want to go back to my home universe. Travel broadens the mind but too much travel wears the soul. I need a sleeping bag, though, just to see ..."

"There are other universes? What are they like?" you ask, intrigued.

"Much like your one, I reckon. I have a pound note somewhere, I'll bet that you have never seen one of those. I picked up some British Euros somewhere too, though they are less remarkable. Oh – you should go to the library. That's where you can find out about them – sorry, I should have said that first. I've been to Middle Earth, you know."

"You mean that Middle Earth is just another universe?"

"It diverged from our world a long time ago, but yes Tolkein was a traveller like me – most of the writers in there with their strange worlds, they are just doing travelogue writing. Of course, Tolkein made loads of it up – there is no evil Lord Sauron and Mordor is really just a particularly grim suburb of Leeds, but most of the rest is true. There are hobbits."

You are no longer following quite what she is saying. You still have no idea why she needs a sleeping bag. She seems to be warming to you and that makes you nervous. You only came in here for a hot drink and a sit down. It is a long drive to Brecon and it will soon be dark. This nonsense that the woman is talking, her story has no beginning, middle and end, it is all jumbled up. It cannot be true.

*   *   *   *   *

The questions are always the same and, frankly, Laura is becoming tired of them.

Rob and Dav are two mates setting off for the source of the River Severn. They must travel about twelve miles from Llanidloes and they have been consulting their maps across a table in the café when Laura approaches them. They ask the same questions.

"How do you know if a universe is different?"

Laura is prepared for this one. Her battered coat shows the hallmarks of having travelled far, but its pockets are deep. She reaches into one and pulls out a banknote.

"You are still using banknotes here, aren't you?" she asks with that same seriousness that worries so many of the people to whom she speaks.

Rob and Dav's confusion confirms to her that plastic-only currency is not part of this world. Good, her world still uses banknotes or, at least, she thinks that it does. She has travelled a lot and home is starting to feel a little like a foggy memory in her mind.

"This banknote," she explains, "comes from a universe where Queen Elizabeth II died in 2003. She is still Queen here, right? Nod if ... okay, good. Normal thing, ten pound note, Jane Austen on one side, on the other ..."

Rob and Dav stare at the strange figure on the reverse side of the note. The note looks genuine but for the picture of an old man holding an orb and sceptre and looking especially glum.

"King Charles III," announces Laura grandly. As the two friends hold and inspect the currency, Laura adds the same insistent question that she asks everyone, "Can I borrow a sleeping bag?"

*   *   *   *   *

The reactions are always the same. In fact, Laura has learned just how predictable human beings are. Truth be told, if you have a choice of going left or right at the end of the road, then ninety-nine times out of a hundred you choose right. She used to see this as immensely comforting, for instance she had only been to one version of the universe where nuclear war devastated human civilisation in the early 1960s. That is how she realised the importance of the café, it was one of very few things that had survived that one.

Generally, human beings have bumbled along in the same way. This is one reason why it is so hard to find her way home. Occasionally she seems to find somewhere that looks right, but when she finally tries the key in the door to her flat, an irate homeowner chases her way. The only true way to know is to find a sleeping bag.

Meryl Meredith, who used to work in an office that made computers and before then used to be known as 'MM' and before then used to be teased for her name, reacted exactly the same way as everyone else does.

"If this is all true, why haven't I heard about this before?"

"Why would you? Some of us have used it for technical advances sure – you know those great leaps forward in science or technology that makes someone billions and changes everything? They tend to be travellers taking things from elsewhere. Mostly though, who would listen? I have told my story so many times ... no wonder so many of us become writers."

"Writers?" asked Mrs M, who had been intrigued by the idea of a universe in which her husband had not left her for a younger woman on Christmas Day.

"Didn't I say that? Sorry, I forget."

"What, like Star Wars and things?"

"No, don't be silly, Star Wars is made up. No-one believes that nonsense!"

There is the reaction that Laura dreads - the polite smile, the change of topic to the weather and the loss of warmth in the face. Mrs Meredith would not be lending her a sleeping bag.

* * * * *

The handshake is always the same. At one point Laura decided that she would one day meet the same person in alternative universes and impress them with her knowledge of them. She always goes to the toilets and puts her right hand under the hand-dryer. Everyone will talk to someone with a warm handshake. 'I'm Laura Clift' she announces to people with her hand outstretched and they feel the need to give their full name as they shake it. Be honest, it is what you did when she offered you her hand.

She has never met Danny Challinor before but they are having a good conversation now. Danny is bored – not just with this cold Saturday in Llanidloes but with everything. He saw no prospects in his town, nothing to do and nowhere to go – even if there was somewhere to go, you could never afford to go there. Then a man from the army arrived at his school and told him that the army could take him all over the world and teach him new skills. Now he is training, but still dreaming of a different life.

Laura has always found that people with little love for their universe listen the most intently to her. Just as the rich never quite appreciate what it means to be poor, so those who have much to be thankful for in their life never quite appreciate what it means to have little to be thankful for. The idea of a different universe appeals to Danny.

"These other worlds, then," he is saying, "what are they like?"

"Some are very different, some are very the same. Sometimes you learn all sorts of weird things. For instance, do you know the port of Fishguard in south-west Wales? In my home universe, the harbour wall there was built at the wrong angle, three degrees to one side. Big ships could never get in, so it never developed as a big port. I went to another universe where they never made that mistake and so Fishguard became the hub of trade and – sadly – slavery and not Liverpool. Liverpool was this little cargo depot for Manchester and Pembrokeshire was rich on trade."

"I meant more like are there big wars and things?"

"Sometimes. All I really know is that this café is always in the same place in each universe and that I come in here and think about travelling somewhere new, walk out and I am there. I think some people can control it – that's the point about libraries, those writers could control where they went, I think."

"Yeah, well, like I said, I don't go into libraries. So you have been doing this for a long time?"

"Too long."

"It sounds so cool, though. Why a sleeping bag, mind?"

"Oh, it is cool for a while, but I miss ... well, look, think of it this way. In some universes I own a flat. I go and look for it first, that's always the first thing. I get to the door and I am so damn nervous about whether it is mine."

"Does that key fit in every universe?"

"No, but luckily I am really predictable and in most universes I have left a spare under the ... hold on, I'm not telling you that!"

"Could I go with you? What if we left together?"

"Tried that. Sorry to say I ended up alone and never saw the bloke again. I can stay in the same universe if I want ... and that's what I want when I find my home universe. To stay. Why move?"

"Couldn't think of anything worse ... but why the sleeping bag, you're still not making sense."

"My PIN number and so on are less predictable. So what happens if I have no flat and no money? I'm sleeping under the market square building down there. I learned pretty damn quickly that there is very little variation in shops and things open around here after five. I hit on leaving a sleeping bag behind the cistern in the toilets here – remember, the café is always the same. Genius! Then I knew that I could always find somewhere to sleep. I have slept rough, I won't lie. Once on a supermarket roof, once in a public toilet ... it's not a glamorous life, you know."

"You must occasionally get the currency ..."

"I do sometimes, sometimes. But it was when I was using the sleeping bag that I discovered the one thing I always knew was right."

"What?"

"Well," and at this point Laura looks around and lowers her voice in case anyone overhears and thinks that she is crazy – as if everything else she has said to date makes perfect sense, "it never feels quite right in a different universe. You know how you see a face or a place and recognise it, you know, it is just right. They say love at first sight is like that. It's the same when you snuggle down in a sleeping bag. In the right one, you jump up and down, wiggle about, bend yourself into the right position but then ... you sleep beautifully."

"Like getting back to your own bed – done that after training camps."

"Yes, yes, yes, just like your own bed after travelling for months. You know it when you feel it. I realised that all I had to do was get my sleeping bag somewhere discrete and I would know – I WOULD KNOW – if it felt right. Stupid isn't it? It's not the people or the places or the money or the possessions, it's a warm, snugly feeling as you fall asleep that defines your own universe. It never feels right elsewhere."

Danny is looking at Laura with a confused expression on his face. He had called in at the café on his way home for a hot drink and never thought that he would be pulled into this crazy story. Laura had a pleasant, if slightly wild, smile and a warm handshake. He thought that his mother would have approved of a warm handshake.

"My sleeping bag is back home, but it's only five minutes away."

"I don't know if I can leave and stay in the same reality. I am not very happy with this one, although you're the first ..."

"Stay here. I'll get it, then you can try it out somewhere – I don't know, they must have a back room ..."

"They do, the café is ..."

"Yeah yeah yeah, I'll be back."

"Be quick, Danny, it's getting late."

Danny Challinor goes out into Llanidloes and breaks into a run. The High Street is busy with Christmas shoppers hurrying back to their cars and he has to push through them. He has trained long enough to be fit and even in army boots, he can pick up speed. He is not sure why, but it is the first thing that has made sense to him in some time. All he can see in front of him is his sleeping bag, standard training issue, hanging in his wardrobe. He would help Laura out, maybe she could find a way for him to go somewhere with her. Maybe the reason that he always felt so out of place in this world was because he too had the travelling talent. He laughed out loud as he bounded around another corner and dodged the X525 bus to Aberystwyth coming the other way.

He has crossed another three roads now and is nearing his house. The night is starting to fall and he realises that he must be quick. His hand is already in his pocket feeling for the key before he reaches the front door. His heart is pounding.

An awkward fumble with the door conquered, Danny darts into the hallway and starts up the stairs.

"Daniel!" comes the call from a room downstairs, "Take your boots off before you come in – how many times?"

"Mam!" replies Danny, running back down the stairs, "I am not here for long, this is urgent."

"You're later than you said you would be," observes Danny's mother as she appears in the hallway.

"Sorry Mam, I stopped at the café and there's this girl there ..."

"And is she going to walk the dog for you?"

"Mam!" complains Danny again, "I need to see her again!"

"I am sure that you do, but you said that you'd walk Freddie when you got in and look at the poor thing, he is crossing all four legs wanting to go out!"

Danny looks at Freddie, a grumpy-looking bull terrier and decides that there is nothing less like a poor thing but no, no dogs allowed in the café, he needs to go back alone.

"Nan's here for tea, don't forget. I thought that you were going to help?"

"Oh yes, Nan. Look I just need to get one thing, then I'll come straight back."

"Like you were going to come straight back today? You can always text or message this girl or something later. She'll still be there."

"No, she won't be."

"Oh Daniel, in years to come you'll look back and realise that not everything in life is the end of the universe. Teenagers, I don't know ..."

"Mam!"

"Daniel Simon Challinor, you are going to walk the dog and be glad of it. Look, that's Nan's car now, I don't want you playing up now."

Danny's mother disappears further into the house and Danny looks on with horror as his Nan starts to make her slow way up to the house from the road. There is a smell of roasting food in the air too. There is no doubt about it, he has to find a way out.

Now he is making calculations. He can grab the sleeping bag and be out the door with the dog without too much trouble. He can talk to Nan and then still be back there within half an hour – tie the dog up in the street, no-one will bother him. Get in and talk to Laura, she can try the sleeping bag and ... and then he feels sad as he realises that then the most intriguing day of his life would be at an end.

Nan to the left of him, mother in front, dog somewhere to the side, his strategy is planned in detail.

* * * * *

Danny stares at the empty table. Everything else looks the same in there, but there is no Laura. The waitresses are closing up around him.

"The girl! The girl who was here, where ... where is she?" he angrily demands.

The waitresses are in no mood to be polite to an angry young man with an army haircut and a sleeping bag.

"We threw her out," says one of them, "she was driving the customers nuts, always asking for ... err ... a sleeping bag, actually."

The waitresses are looking at the sleeping bag swinging from Danny's right hand, its cord clenched in his determined fist. They are giggling, only a little, but enough to annoy Danny.

"What have you done?"

"Threw her out. She was begging people for cups of tea. Then after you left before and we tried to make her pay, she offered this – bloody cheek!"

Danny takes the banknote in his hand and stares at the image of King Charles III on the reverse. He has no idea why Laura wanted to stay here when there must be so many more exciting alternatives.

"She did say that she was waiting for someone to return," comments the shortest of the three thoughtfully.

"I thought that she was making that up," says another.

"She probably was," says the third, "we attract all the nutters here."

"Yeah," they all agree with a laugh, "it is always the same in this café."

Conversations with Rioters

[This was written in the aftermath of the urban riots that took place in England in August 2011. Young people were wrongly blamed for much of the violence and this led to a rush of generalisations and ill-thought out policies from our political leaders].

Given all the controversy over the riots in England (and the small outbreaks of rioting in Wales that went unreported - doubtless the same happened in Scotland too), I thought that it was time to talk to some rioters.

I spoke to Chantelle Barry from Bristol. She is one of those young people who has been criticised very heavily in media coverage of the events. Aged seventeen she has two children and was happy to take part in some recent theft to supplement her income. I asked her to explain her choices in life -

"It's so true," she told me, "The age of sixteen is a very bewildering time and you have to decide how you want your life to be. Living in an inner city part of Bristol where there are generations of unemployment and little hope of improvement, I thought that I probably had three possibilities. I could take on some non-executive company director roles - I was looking at international pharmaceutical companies mostly - or I could become a High Court judge or I could start a family. Of course, it's easy to see now but if I only had stayed on at school without the means to support myself and done some of that judging, I could have a big house out in Clifton by now".

Chantelle is not alone in blaming herself. Her friend, Kylie Barry (no relation) puts it clearly - "With my dead end education in a school that had written me off as bad for the League Tables before I was 14 and which therefore rarely bothered any encouragement for me taking GCSEs, I really should have become an entrepreneur or at the very least read Politics, Philosophy and Economics at Oxford. The opportunities have been handed to me on a plate and I have just selfishly pushed them away. I have no idea why I felt a failure, I can only think it was bad parenting."

In London, I caught up with Tim Barry from Hackney, who had also been involved in disturbances last week. He told me about the problems that there were with local role models for young people.

"The thing is this," said Tim leaning nonchalantly against a stack of stolen TVs now reduced to clear on GumTree.com, "we really do have bad role models around here. If you're really unlucky you'll get a teacher in school who wants to inspire you or a youth worker at the youth club who wants to encourage you. I used to go down to my local gym where an ex-pro did boxing lessons to channel your anger. What a load of bollocks - thank goodness Cameron is cutting back on this stuff. The people who inspire me are politicians, the police and the people who lead businesses like Vodafone. I can relate to these people. You only have to look at how closely the police and the press co-operated on the phone hacking thing to see that these are people who have principles that they stick to. Safe".

His friend Phil Barry (no relation) who is visiting him from Croydon and must therefore be in a rival gang agrees with this analysis. "The thing that people don't get about the police is that they are doing a vital job," he explains.

"When I am walking down the street and they stop me for no reason because I am young and therefore must be up to no good, I really respect them and the job they are doing. If it's after dark and they go through my pockets and tell me I must be a burglar, I get this tremendous sense of admiration and respect for them and their work. Planting guns and drugs on people to get an arrest? It's all part of the hard work they do. Only more police will improve things round here."

It is pretty clear that the problems on England's streets have been caused by people in local communities who want to do dangerous things like 'inspire' young people. It is an argument backed up by Simone Barry, who until recent government cuts ran a youth work centre in Birmingham.

"What we need is more police and less youth workers," she explains. "You hear how much young people look up to the police. If they are going to riot, they need to hear the threatening voice of a police officer through a megaphone to make them stop, the last thing they want to hear is someone from their community who they see around the place every day working to improve things and who has personally helped them at a difficult time in their life, telling them to stop."

"Many young people tell me how much they look up to David Cameron and how much they respect him because he understands their background. We need more people like David Cameron telling us how to run our neighbourhood and less from local people who think that just because they know an area, its inhabitants and its problems, this somehow makes them more knowledgeable than Mr Cameron and his friends."

It is these kind of voices that have helped form the new Conservative policy. More police on the streets, a clampdown aimed at young people, continued cuts to voluntary and statutory youth services and an exasperation as to why people do not admire and look up to their MPs, police, corporate business leaders and others in the public eye. It is just the right recipe to get England back on its feet again. This 'me first' selfish attitude has to change and change it will, at least the next riots will be long after Mr Cameron has retired on his meager public service pension which has been cut back to a ... oh hold on, sorry, pensions for MPs have not been cut back at all, which must be because we admire them so much for taking on the 'me first' attitude.

A Word in Time

"I am very lucky to be joined here by Professor Gareth Humphries from the University of South Wales. Professor, I am sure that on this night when we are discussing sci-fi and I suppose the science part of that rather than the fiction, people must ask you about this kind of subject a lot."

Gareth Humphries smiled and acknowledged the audience in the television studio with a small wave. He knew that there were two reasons why he was here. The first was that the University was undersubscribed for its science courses last year and this was part of a strategy to generate more students and therefore course fees through publicity. Staff were supposed to be more 'cool' and 'approachable' now.

The second was that Gareth had been part of a minor one hit wonder group some twenty years before. His schoolfriend Jonjo Minto had roped him into being in a backing band for a single that should never have gone anywhere. Instead it went on to the radio, the internet and for an agonisingly long, hot summer from every car or shop that he walked past.

Gareth was not a happy minor pop star and he always heard that moment after two minutes thirty seconds when he was slightly late coming in with the backing vocal. He hated hearing that mistake over and over. Most of all he had wanted to go back to being a student.

"Did you bring the bass along?" quipped the host of the show.

"No Earl, I thought that I would leave that at home this time."

Gareth had been asked that in most interviews and he could have sworn that there was an audible sigh of disappointment from the audience each time. He had a PhD now. People with a PhD should not be asked if they have a bass guitar. At some point in the interview they would show a picture of him in the band. Some things could be predicted. However much he wanted to grimace, he smiled.

"Okay well, as you know, tonight we are celebrating the return of 'Moonflight' - I think ... I think ... someone can correct me if I am wrong here ... my producer Graham is just off the screen there and he is nodding ... this is now the second-longest sci-fi programme on TV. Wow, yes, applause, I think."

The audience were applauding as requested. Professor Gareth Humphries smiled weakly.

"Now Professor, we wanted to put some questions to you about the science used in these programmes. Perhaps you can help?"

"Sure thing Earl," replied Gareth, thinking that perhaps it sounded a little too 'cool'. If only he had not had his hair cut last week.

Earl Carter looked straight at the camera now, "And we are now going to answer some of the big questions - let's start with what I know many of you are interested in, time travel. Professor, is it possible?"

"I'm sorry to disappoint you Earl, but the answer is definitely 'no'."

"That is a disappointment," said the host, a smile twinkling towards the camera, "there are a few people I'd like to go back and look up. What's the problem with it, is it that you boffins just haven't found how to make it work?"

The Professor sighed and smiled. He remembered being told not to show nerves. It was all on autocue anyway. That had been a strange revelation to him, the whole show was pretty much scripted. He had given his answers to the questions in advance and the words appeared on the camera in the centre of the stage. All that crazy improvisation that the Earl was known for? Threre was a whole writing team for that. Still, his host had warned him that the autocue had been throwing up odd words for a little while and just to read what it said, no matter what. Clearly improvisation was not tolerated. These thoughts returned to the Professor as he stared down the lens of the central camera.

"No Earl, we are all quite azo with it, but it is more that it is a physical impossibility."

He looked over at the host, who gave a wink cleverly hidden from the camera. He was saying not to worry over what an 'azo' was, perhaps it was some street slang the writers had thrown in, who knows, just go with it that wink said.

"Now that sounds a tizo bit defensive to me," read Earl from the autocue – you had to hand it to him, he was very skilled in making rehearsed lines sound spontaneous – "why do you think that we have all these stories about it then?"

The Professor paused to ponder a better answer than he had given to the writing team. It was a pause just long enough to draw a bit of panic into Earl Carter's eyes and from behind his dark fringe, he flashed a look of 'talk!' to his guest.

"Some may call my answer streethious," was the start of the sentence he read out, but now the Professor decided to add his own words in, "what does streethious actually mean, Earl?"

Earl Carter had not become the leading light of early evening television without some knowledge of how to deal with the unexpected. He barely skipped a beat.

"It means like street-talk, you know, 'hey, you are being a bit streethious'. Sorry folks, the Professor is not quite up on the language of today."

There was a glance to the camera, some laughter from the audience, that trademark smile and glint in the eye – the Professor decided to stay with the script.

"Well, to give you an answer *in totales*, we are travelling forwards in time every day. 24 hours at a time is our only progress. We cannot speed that up, we cannot slow that down. What is done is done and only exists in our minds, what has not yet happened does not exist – it would be like trying to walk over bridge that has not been built yet."

"'Sqip man!' as they say, that's a sad thought."

"I think that we all have regrets, things that we would like to go back and change and the stories reflect that. The real challenge is to get it right first time around, live a lotel life if you know what I mean."

"First time, eh? Well, it's funny you should say that, we happen to have a picture of your first career here ..."

As the laughter rang out about his youthful hairstyle, Professor Gareth Humphries wondered what 'lotel' meant. He had always been interested in language but these weird words had been a feature of the show for some weeks. Apparently younger viewers loved them and were adopting them as part of their language. It was predicted that they would be in the dictionary by the next edition. Ec, as people were now saying. Wise opinion pieces appeared in newspapers to condemn this, only making it all the more popular.

*   *   *   *   *

"How are we today, Mr Humphries?" asked Lesley as she opened the curtains.

"I don't know how **we** are, but **I** am fine thank you, Lesley," replied the Professor from his sofa, "I have told you why I tolerate your visits."

Lesley walked across to the sofa to address him directly. She was one of those people who have only one professional setting - perky cheeriness -

154

and she delivered it in a no-nonsense Glaswegian accent which made for a frightening combination.

"You tolerate my visits because after the last incident the doctors told you that you had to have them. We all need checking up on from time to time, don't we?"

Professor Humphries nodded towards the computer set up to the side of the sofa, "You know it is the games I am interested in."

Lesley had walked into his kitchen while he was talking. He could hear her checking the medicine cabinet and probably his fridge as well. In a moment she would ask if he was cooking with salt still. He sighed. He could still get about, he could still move, there was no need for a care home yet, but he had to admit that the years had slowed him down. To be honest, there were more than seventy years packed into his ageing bones now.

"I hope that that salt cellar has not been used," shouted a uniformed voice from the kitchen.

Gareth had not accepted that he had slowed down at all in the years since that TV interview at the height of his academic career. There were few victories that the day would bring him now.

"How are you finding the stairlift?"

"As a reminder of who I no longer am."

"Let's have a look at these bandages, shall we?"

Gareth sighed. He was not sure if Lesley practised this slightly patronising professional detachment or whether it was just her way of coping. He lifted up his trouser leg so she could inspect the bandages on his right leg. He thought that he might use the moment to be philosophical.

"It's nothing like you think, you know. I still wake up and wonder why I am not twenty but somehow this body – this body – will not do what I want it to do. The stairlift now walks for me where once I could walk."

Lesley looked up at him and smiled, "But you're here now, aren't you?"

"Ah, what would you know? You're still young."

"I've two small children, I don't feel young anymore!"

"Okay, okay, but put it this way maybe. I saw a play by a youth theatre a few years ago – from Wrexham they were. They played three people sitting in a care home. Do you know what they kept saying? 'I've had a good life, me'. That was what they thought old people did, we are supposed to sit around thinking about whether we have had a good life or not."

"And you don't?"

"Who knows if I have had a good life or not? I tried to fill it with what interested me, I tried to be decent to people but no-one's perfect. We all mess up. Even the person you admire the most messes up. The person you despise the most has done some good for someone. These young people want life to be like a fortune cookie where a neat little bit of wisdom falls out at the end. Well, I'm none the bloody wiser."

Lesley had stopped looking at the bandage and was sitting back and looking at him. She had lovely brown eyes, he thought to himself. Those brown eyes had probably helped her get those two children.

"I've found out something about you," she said unexpectedly.

Gareth stiffened and it caused a shot of pain through his bandaged leg.

"You're going to ask me if I've got that bloody bass guitar, aren't you?"

"What bass guitar?"

"Oh."

Lesley shook her head and returned to unwrapping the bandage as she spoke. He was unsure if she was going to apply a new bandage or just tighten the old one. He looked away as she talked.

"I found out that you were an expert on time travel. One of the girls back at the clinic said that she had seen you on an old recording of a chat show. You said that time travel was impossible but you still devoted your life to studying it."

"Well ...," said Professor Humphries feeling a little academic pride, "it's true that I did, but I said in that interview that it's impossible. Besides, who would want to travel in time?"

Lesley sat back again and this time it looked as though she had finished with the bandaged leg so Gareth rolled his trouser back down.

"I would."

"What would you do?"

"Well … I think that I would go back and see my parents before their kids were born. I'd like to see what they were like. I'd tell them not to panic, they would get grandkids one day!"

"You turn up on their doorstep as you are now – a thirtysomething woman – they wouldn't recognise you. You don't change when you travel through time. In fact, if you leave at one point and then spend months in the past then you end up going back having aged more than the people who didn't travel."

"Politics then. I'd go back and change something significant."

"Oh no, not another holocaust preventer. Can't be done - that act took the compliance of millions, one person cannot change a massive historical event like that."

"How about the Scottish devolution referendum of 1979? Long before my time I know, but I read that had Scotland got its own Parliament then, before the North Sea oil came online then we could have had a great social democracy and not Margaret Thatcher giving it to all her cronies."

"Ha! You know the important stuff!"

"You've not gathered the whole Glasgow thing, then?"

Lesley was laughing, not something she normally did around patients. Gareth smiled, sensing for a moment that his normal adversary in health care was softening.

"What about the future, then?" she asked, "I'd go forwards in time. I'd meet my own grandchildren. See if Dan ever gets that book published. See if that bloody Moonflight show he watches is ever cancelled. It's still going, you know, that was long-running when I was born!"

"Future hasn't happened yet, you can't go there."

"Oh ... well, if you are intent on ruining all my dreams then I am going to take your blood pressure. If you can't dream about the impossible, there isn't much point, is there?"

Lesley took the blood pressure cuff out of her bag while Gareth rolled up his sleeve. She had been his health visitor for long enough that they both knew the tests to do and how they were done.

"You know what keeps me going?" asked Gareth, suddenly aware that in this visit they had moved from 'how are we?' to the point of life, "I would find some victory, some way to show that though my body is declining, I can still do it, I can still affect someone's life."

"And breathe normally."

"Beating you at Scrabble, for instance."

"I told you – I was Glasgow City Champion five years running. I know every Xi, every Fe and every Qat that I need to win."

The Professor pulled a small computer over from the other side of the sofa with his free arm. He pressed some buttons and the screen filled with Scrabble boards.

"Five games and I am in the lead in all of them," he announced smugly.

Did he hear Lesley swear under her breath? He smiled to himself, she really did not like being beaten. Underneath the breezy professional exterior, this woman loved being in control of her life and knowing that she was winning.

"Are you sure that you have been resting that leg?" she asked.

"Yes," he lied.

"Well ..., okay then, that's me done. I'll come back next week to check up on you again. We are having a bit of a shake-up in the home visit service, so you may only get me fortnightly in future, nothing's settled."

"Would you come in to play Scrabble with me every week though?"

The question caused them both to stop and pause. Gareth was surprised by his need to say it, she was surprised by him asking.

"If you aren't afraid of losing, mind you ..."

"Let's have a look at these games, then," she demanded.

"Hmm ... first one," said the nurse, studying the computer intently, her eyes flicking along rows of letters, her mind searching a large vocabulary to make the killer move, "hold on, what's AZO?"

"Perfectly good word. You know the computer only accepts words in the dictionary. Been in circulation for about thirty years."

"I'm not convinced, but let's look at the second ... ah, this one. I'm not convinced with this one because you played STREETHIOUS out of where I had played STREET."

"Again, it was accepted. It's the quality of language being 'street', I believe ... you can check it. Or, of course, if you can't get back into the game after that, you can resign."

"Never. I don't know about your vocab, you keep saying that it's academic language but it's nothing that I've heard. I'm ahead in this next one, but I don't like TOTALES or SQIP. You seem to be just playing the obscure words."

"I have a big vocabulary. You know the rule is that if it has been used publicly and can be sourced from the internet's vast range of language then it is in the online dictionary."

Lesley stood back up and started to collect up her belongings, "Give me the web address and I'll play at home. I might have more of a clue when I am not on my rounds. Hmm ... thank goodness you can't play TIZO on that board."

"TIZO. Damn, I forgot I'd set that up," muttered the Professor.

"So, we'll see how you are next week, shall we?"

Lesley had returned to her professional, slightly patronising approach. Gareth sighed, he had almost had her beaten. He would do still and that would be his small victory.

She was looking at the screen again, "There's no word LOTEL, is there?"

The Professor studied the screen. He had decided that as a gift he would let her have that one.

"Try it next week," he said.

After Lesley left, the Professor (retired) would sit in that stairlift and make the journey up the stairs to the spare room. No-one had ever believed him, but now – bandaged leg or not – he would make the journey that gave him the most pleasure. In one pocket of his long overcoat would be a list of all the words that he needed to keep his lead in the Scrabble games, the other would be his directions for interfering with the autocue unnoticed.

One time, just out of sight, he had heard his younger self talking to the Earl – long before the scandal that brought that star to earth of course – but talking like someone who thought that he knew it all, just as he would have thought at forty that his twenty year old self had misplaced cockiness too.

He might have aged, he might need to cheat like this, but he could still have his small victories ... by twenty three points in the last game.

A Touch of Mischievous Sarcasm

[The first book that I wrote was 'The Slightly New Adventures of Lucy Roadnight'. In it, two young women drift apart after they leave university in Cardiff and struggle to adjust to being adults against a backdrop of the usual weirdness that I like. Lucy works in the recycling department of Cardiff Council, specialising in complaints ('People like shouting at you,' as her boss explains to her in her annual appraisal). This chapter deals with Lucy's progress in the workplace].

The sound of Lucy's alarm clock on a Monday morning started a race that always ended with her crossing a finishing line at her desk, just in time to start work for another week. The starting gun was fired by the clock's annoying electronic ringing at seven fifteen in the morning. Some mornings Lucy reacted as though it were a starting gun by her ear. There was no 'snooze' button, though a gap of up to ten minutes was allowed in her plans for lying in bed thinking 'not Monday again' or for recovering from a weird dream where she had a strange desire to shout the number 38 in her sleep.

At 7.25 a.m., she would make her way to the kitchen to start the kettle boiling and, while it was boiling, would quickly step in to the shower in the bathroom. Still washing the sleep from her eyes, she would return to the kitchen and have her breakfast set out with a big mug of coffee by 7.35 a.m. Switching on the radio to hear the latest news was an optional extra, so long as it did not delay her from the move from eating to dressing that was due to start at 7.45 a.m.

It was not a smart workplace, but 'no jeans or trainers' was a definite rule. Lucy never had her clothes laid out ready in the morning but found that it was an easy choice to make and could grab a smart casual dress or a pair of trousers and a top without having to think about it too much. Make-up would be minimal and she had never been one for complicated arrangements of her hair every morning. The deadline was to be out of the door washed, breakfasted and dressed by 8.15 a.m.

The walk from Lucy's flat to the station in the suburban backroads was a nondescript fifteen minutes next to neatly-arranged houses and front gardens. The next checkpoint was on the platform, which she had to be standing on by 8.30 a.m. so that the train could roll in to meet her at 8.32 a.m.

If the train was agreeable to its part in Lucy's timetable, then she would be leaving Cardiff Queen Street station by 8.45 a.m. She liked to think that she stepped on to the commuter train a dazed caterpillar and emerged a resplendent butterfly, ready to tackle another day and dazzle her work colleagues with her competence. The truth was more likely to be that she had stood on the train for ten minutes and yawned loudly several times.

This particular Monday was the day for the monthly figures and targets to be reported at her workplace and now that Lucy had a small team to lead, she would be talking to them about their performance. In her head, she started to rehearse what she would say. Ten minutes walk along Queen Street, turn right and along the Victorian terraces of Park Place to her distinctly more modern office building. Up the stairs to the second floor – no lift, that is lazy – and sit down at the desk. Each desk has a phone and each phone has a clock, time on the clock – 8.56 a.m. This first tired glance at the clock was the race's finishing line – from clock to clock in one hour and forty-one minutes, an uncelebrated triumph for the modern athlete / butterfly. On this Monday it would mean three minutes to read the month's figures, prepare a few thoughts accordingly and then take them into the team meeting.

The Council offices on Park Place were a post-war addition to an otherwise scenic street. Inside they had been refurbished to be 'open plan' with only low barriers dividing each team and each department. Lucy was still not completely sure which Council services were delivered from some floors of the building, but there was a definite territorial feel to the place and dark stories were told of people who ventured on to the third floor looking for a coffee machine and never returned. There were meeting rooms scattered across each floor, but they had see-through walls to encourage 'transparency'. Whenever Lucy thought about this she could hear a well-paid architect claim that 'the very materials of the walls give expression to the ideal'. What it did mean was that lip-readers were highly prized for their ability to obtain gossip from watching other people's meetings. The Departmental Director was the only person who had a traditional office in a room with a door that closed. This did add a certain irony to his constant declarations in his monthly e-mails that 'my door is always open'.

Lucy liked her team. There were three others of them – Sandra, mother to three children and the team, who worked part-time around her children's schooling and then the two younger team members, Simon and Cerys, both from Barry and both no more than a few years out of school.

"I've booked the meeting room by the kitchen and I'll just get a round of drinks – everyone's usual?" asked Sandra, picking up a black triangular tray which would hold enough plastic cups to cater for everyone.

It was rare for Sandra to be in at – Lucy peered at her phone - 9.04 a.m. but the monthly nine o'clock meeting was an exception. There was also the feeling of job insecurity in the air and they would probably want to know what she knew. Lucy knew nothing and wondered if she should admit this.

"I'll meet you there," said Sandra as she disappeared with the tray.

"Phones on divert to general waste, please," said Lucy and walked towards the meeting room, pausing only to pick up a red, a yellow and a green pencil from a desk drawer and the print out of the month's statistics from her in-tray. 'Be a butterfly!' she told herself.

Behind her, Simon and Cerys were discussing their weekends. Simon was re-iterating a point that he made to Cerys earlier, "No, he definitely said that her name was Cerys, she was from

Barry and she was really dirty in bed, that has to be you!"

"It wasn't me!" Cerys was protesting with some enjoyment of the discussion.

Lucy felt moved to interrupt them – "What does it actually mean to be 'dirty in bed'?" she asked, "I mean, does it mean that you don't wash? Or is it that you don't wash your sheets? I've sometimes wondered."

Cerys started a reply, "You know, dirty in bed, it means like, you know ..."

Simon raised his eyebrows at her, clearly waiting for her to explain what sexual acts she considered as falling into the 'dirty' category. Cerys laughed at his eagerness and then stopped her explanation.

Lucy realised that she had crossed two lines by involving herself in this conversation. Firstly, she was their Manager and this immediately meant that she was different to them and was not going to be included in the jokey banter. Then there was her age – she was not that much older than them surely, but this was a huge gap for people of their age. What was Simon - 20, 21 – Cerys no more than 19? For them, people in their twenties had already become old and there was no point trying to have some kind of connection with them. Besides, the way that the two of them flirted, it was a wonder to Lucy that they had not simply 'got a room' as the saying went and not a glass-walled meeting room either. Lucy had always been one of those people who thought that people attracted to each other should act on it.

Sandra was waiting in the meeting room with two coffees, one tea and a plastic cup full of bright green soup.

"Pull up a chair," said Lucy, as they sat around the table. "You all know why we're here. I also have a few things to talk about and you might want to ask a few questions. First thing – you should have seen the memo from the Director. No-one involved in Complaints is to use the phrase 'we are experiencing a high volume of calls at the moment' as this may give people the impression that a lot of people are complaining."

"A lot of people are complaining," interjected Sandra, only too aware of what the economy drive to only collect general waste once a fortnight instead of once a week had done for the general level of complaints and queries.

"As I say, it is more important what impression we are giving," repeated Lucy, and then added with a touch of mischievous sarcasm, "remember, it's not about the service, it's about the targets."

Lucy noticed that no-one questioned her sarcastic mission statement. She moved on to talk about targets.

"As you know, we run the targets on a traffic light system – red for failing to hit the target, amber if we are close and green if we are hitting the target. This is known as the RAG system."

Lucy waited for Simon to mutter, "We're on the RAG this month!" as he did every month. He also giggled at this every month. No-one else ever did.

Cerys raised her hand, which looked a little strange in what Lucy was hoping to be an informal meeting. Lucy nodded at her and Cerys held up a set of papers that she had brought with her. "We don't have colours on our print outs, so we can't see what's RAG and what's not."

Simon passed Lucy a copy of his print out as proof – "It's an economy drive, boss, no more colour cartridges in the printers. You have to ask for specific permission to print in colour."

"I heard that we're going to be limited in how much black and white we can print out too," added Sandra, sipping her bright green soup.

Lucy stared at the grey columns on the paper in front of her. "Could we maybe take the dark grey as red, the light grey as amber and the medium grey to be green?" she asked in some despair.

"Is it true we're going to be limited in the amount of print outs we do?" asked Cerys.

"I heard it was because one of the Senior Planning Officers was printing pornographic pictures on the colour printers and it used up the Council's entire stock of green ink," added Sandra helpfully.

"What kind of porn uses up all the green ink?" asked Simon thoughtfully.

This was also Lucy's question, but she decided to make a Managerial attempt to drive the meeting back along the right road. "I believe that any allegations have been dealt with," she announced, "but we do know that there are difficult times ahead."

"Is it true that we're being merged with food waste?" asked Sandra.

"That just wouldn't work," exclaimed Cerys, "you can't mix recycling and food waste, that's why people have different bins..."

"I know nothing," announced Lucy, deciding to go for honesty, "I do know that we have been very successful in recycling in dealing with people's enquiries and that 44% of all rubbish in the city is now recycled. Although the plan is to push on towards 80%, there is less need for so many people dedicated to recycling."

"They'll pick on the part-timers first," said Sandra gloomily.

"No, it'll be the youngest – always the youngest first!" said Cerys.

"It'll be all of us," added Simon, joining the general mood of despondency.

"We'll fight any cuts, you know! We'll strike!" declared Sandra.

"Are you a member of a Union?" asked Lucy, sensing that she knew the answer.

"No," replied Sandra slightly sheepishly.

"Well then, you won't be striking. It might be the Team Leaders anyway or natural wastage from ... err ... across all waste. I would say that you put general rubbish, recycling, garden waste and food waste into one department with a smaller overall team and only one Team Leader. In fact, I would see the whole building being slimmed down into one contact centre. It's happening in a lot of other local authorities – we might even end up merging with the Vale or the Rhondda and providing a wider service."

"Or being 'outsourced' to a private company, I would bet," added Sandra unhelpfully again, "Some business that over-promises on targets and under-deliverers on results and then is rewarded with another government contract."

"Is there anything we can do?" asked Simon, adjusting his glasses and his tie as if he was already at a job interview. "Will you mention it when you next see The Swede?"

"I will. I have to see her later today. I am likely to be going on leave for a couple of weeks pretty much immediately. Please don't read anything into this, a couple of personal things have come up that I need to deal with. Anyway, there won't be any changes immediately. I imagine that there will have to be a very expensive efficiency audit by an external consultant, which will identify ways of saving money that will end up costing a lot of money."

"Could the external consultants recommend not paying large amounts of money to external consultants?" asked Sandra, knowing the answer.

There was silence in the room for a few moments, before Lucy remembered that she had to add, "And don't refer to Sarah as The Swede please,

Simon. She is my Line Manager and you should show her due respect."

Lucy had already booked an appointment to see The Swede later that day. She must remember to call her Sarah.

"And while I think about it, I could have sworn that colour printers use black, red, yellow and blue ink to make all the colours so there is no green ink."

"That's what I'm saying!" exclaimed Cerys, "There is no green ink. All because someone used it to print porn – I have a mate in Planning and he sent me these pictures ..."

Lucy decided that the meeting had achieved all that it could possibly do that morning.

War of the Words

"No-one would have believed in the last years of the nineteenth century that this world was being watched keenly and closely by intelligences greater than man's and yet as mortal as his own; that as men busied themselves about their various concerns they were scrutinised and studied, perhaps almost as narrowly as a man with a microscope might scrutinise the transient creatures that swarm and multiply in a drop of water."

H.G. Wells, 'The War of the Worlds'

REPORT ONE : SUBMITTED 152673 : AGENT 7898 TRANSLATED FROM THE ORIGINAL

I landed in the town of Woking, England as originally intended. Assuming the ages-old galaxy-wide joke of being an 'Estate Agent', I attempted to fit in. I recommend this cover for further expeditions since no-one on the planet seems to have realised that these people are not of their world.

I have discovered some KEY FACTS about the planet and I present these throughout the report.

KEY FACT #1 : The Electric Light Orchestra (or ELO as they were known) released their first album in 1972. The album was simply called 'ELO' in the UK but in the United States, the record company executive in charge of the album asked his secretary to find out the name. She left a note that read 'No answer' to indicate that she had not been able to do so and his misunderstanding when he found the note led to the album being issued as 'No Answer' in the USA.

I became familiar with some of the rituals expected of an Estate Agent. I found a small flat near the canal and started to travel to work at Lines, Swanwick and Harris. On a Friday night we drank at the Hart & Trumpet.

There were promotional offers on vodka, whisky and ... I cannot remember what else, but these may be important details for further study expeditions.

KEY FACT #2 : The FA Cup Final was won in 2008 by Portsmouth FC. Some people are convinced that this is Wimbledon FC but that was earlier in earth time.

There was little more to report about Woking, though I found Monday nights particularly productive as my fellow workers often frequented the Hart & Trumpet for a trial of knowledge.

Branching out, I went to Brighton for one weekend. This is where I encountered sea. I would recommend that we avoid this, it is like a canal but with only one edge and the water chases after you like an angry beast. Luckily the inhabitants of Brighton are also frightened of it as they have built a viewing platform over it.

KEY FACT #3 : There are 206 bones in the human body.

Before leaving, I gained a book of immense knowledge and this has been my guidance in recommending the course of the invasion. I do not believe that we should continue with the invasion until we have mastered all the knowledge contained within it. It certainly seems to be an important to all those who have met on Monday nights and so to act without fully understanding it would be foolish.

I enclose it with this report – 'The Bumper Book of Trivia for Pub Quizzes'.

REPORT ENDS> OFFICIAL STATUS> APPROVED> INVASION DELAYED

REPORT TWENTY-FIVE : SUBMITTED 1906789 : AGENT 8898 TRANSLATED FROM THE ORIGINAL

I started from the basis that the previous report was incorrect and that the agent had become distracted by a deliberate restriction of information by those holding power on planet earth. It may seem incredible to us, but there are many on the planet who think that a knowledge of nuclear fission is irrelevant but that they desperately need to know the nicknames of American Baseball teams. I deliberately targeted the knowledge that I believed would be relevant.

The previous agent was correct that the cover of 'Estate Agent' is ideal, but it is limited to a small part of the planet. I decided that it was important to gain a greater understanding of the planet at large and I was pleased to find that a small amount of money left on the planet by an early agent trying to understand the banking system had gained enough value to finance a trip across the globe.

Naturally I started from the previous agent's base in Woking. However, I found it hard to progress around without something called a 'car'. At its most basic, this converts minerals into energy and poisonous gases. I was shocked by how much the inhabitants of this planet accept this dirtying of their air and, indeed, participate in it. I made slow progress by electric train but then discovered myself in an area where the countryside was being dug up to provide more of the minerals for power. Surely this is unsustainable and there must be a plan for what happens when everything is dug up? I could find no such plan.

Even more troubling was that the production of so much energy was damaging the climate of the planet. This was understood by most intelligent people and yet each new flood, each new storm, each new 'freak' weather event brought strenuous denials from people that there was any connection with the energy production.

I took a boat across a vast sea and on the way met someone who described themselves as an 'environmentalist' from 'Canada'. She told me about the damage being done to 'Alberta tar sands' to remove oil. She also told me that I should visit somewhere called 'South America' where the very trees that provide the oxygen that the inhabitants of the planet breathe were being destroyed. I refused to believe that, it made no sense.

I travelled south, past areas where the sea was used as a dumping ground rather than a natural resource. This 'USA' was an odd country – it was like the first one that I started out in, run by a small group of very rich people and then a larger range of poorer people. And yet even the poorest people had access to a disproportionate share of the planet's resources. It was not that the planet was not abundant – it certainly is, it teems with life – but that this abundance was so shockingly divided between very few and the rest.

By the time I was journeying across a country called 'Africa', I had seen the worst effects of the growing deserts, the lack of water, the exploitation of resources, but I had been drawn to one natural wonder of the planet.

Inhabitants of our own planet will be familiar with the Hellas basin and the tourist industry that has grown up around our lowest point. This planet has a low point too, the Marianas Trench. It is in the sea, but also a wonder of nature since creatures have evolved that can cope with the water pressure at such low depths, often with soft shells. The inhabitants of this planet have noticed this and studied it. I was journeying towards it in the hope that this might be a good example of scientific endeavour by this species.

I stopped and I stop this report with the description that I found on the planet's mass communication tool, the internet. After describing the wonders of this natural feature, the next section is headed 'Potential Use As a Site for Dumping Nuclear Waste'.

There is no need to invade this planet. Its inhabitants will have destroyed it and probably themselves soon enough.

REPORT ENDS> OFFICIAL STATUS> APPROVED> INVASION DELAYED

REPORT THIRTY-THREE : SUBMITTED 2789719 : AGENT 9890{1} TRANSLATED FROM THE ORIGINAL

"As we have updated our processes since the earlier agents reported, I am giving my report verbally and this will be recorded and auto-stored in the archive," said Agent 9890{1}

Agent 08189 sighed – he had been deeply jealous of Agent 9890{1} gaining the planet three assignment, especially after many agents had heard tell of something called 'a fried breakfast' which had caused much joy but also significant long-term health problems for an earlier Agent.

"You may proceed with the report," instructed the Senior Agent, raising a quizzical tentacle.

"Many of the reports that we have received refer to using a language called English. There are many other languages used on the planet and ones called Chinese, Spanish, Arabic and French might also have been chosen. However, as previous agents had concentrated on English, I decided to start from there. The planet's international communication system, the internet, is also useful for using English."

Agent 08189 yawned. The build-up was always the least interesting part of these reports. Still, it was beating the one that concentrated on economic development in a place called 'East Powys'. There were suspicions that that agent had simply made it all up to cover some less reputable activities.

Agent 9890{1} continued without being distracted by the yawn – that {1} distinction was not earned by being thrown off course by a yawn.

"We use the English language as the way of communicating with the inhabitants of the planet and it seems to work in many of the areas that they have designated by different names. Where my research is different from others is that ..."

"Different to," interrupted Agent 08189.

"Different from."

"Different to."

"It hardly matters. Communication is a flexible thing and so long as you have rules ..."

"No, there are rules and they are important. Otherwise how else does anyone know what is right?"

"But is there a right? Surely that is just you imposing your standards on others?"

"Yes, there is a right, I was reading that book by Lynne Truss ..."

"Who is this 'Lynne Truss' ... a political thinker?" interrupted the Senior Agent.

"She's a bully," replied Agent 9890{1}.

"All she wants is to make a no-nonsense approach to grammar rules. There are things that are right and there are things that are wrong. People should know these things."

Agent 9890{1} addressed the Senior Agent directly, "She has written a book of principles for the English Language but what she fails to understand is that communication differs according to situation. If you can make yourself understood, then it is not important whether you know the difference between 'effect' and 'affect'."

"I thought that they were the same word?" asked the Senior Agent.

"Oh my goodness, no!" yelled Agent 08189.

"Tell me about this Lynnetruss creature. She has a book of political philosophy – we can file that with the *Mein Kampf* thing that we picked up a few years ago. What about her army?"

"I came across them on the internet – the planet's communication system – if you break one of the Truss's rules, they will abuse you and humiliate you."

"Interesting ... tell me about some of the inhabitants you were having problems with."

"Err ... no," said Agent 08189, "the inhabitants with whom you were having problems."

"That's what I said."

"No, it's not."

"Ahem ... if I may answer," said Agent 9890{1}, "I made the mistake of writing a quick reply when someone thanked me for something. I said 'Your welcome' and sent it."

"Okay," replied the Senior Agent, "you made a slight error in your typing, easily done, especially when you are pretending to be like those inhabitants and have fingers. So what?"

"Well, so people sent me abuse and angry messages saying that I was stupid. When I tried to defend myself, they said that people like me had to be stopped and I was threatened."

"But people understood what you meant?"

"Oh yes."

"But they still wanted to kill you?"

"Yes."

"What a peculiar race we are dealing with. Any language develops and evolves. A dictionary or a book is like trying to take a picture of a moving vehicle. It shows you a blurred approximation of the language. And so what, people make mistakes – do people really threaten each other over this?"

"All the time."

"Hmm," said the Senior Agent, "so we have a kind of bullying dictatorship over language … with a potential dictator … and bullying acolytes. Well, what an odd situation. The rest of your report?"

Agent 9890{1} paused and rubbed a tentacle. "It was hard to find much more political information on this internet thing. It appeared to be people shouting at each other. I am not quite sure why – they could just stand in a field and shout at birds for all the good it would do."

"What are birds?"

Agent 9890{1} sighed. "I would like to request that I never visit that planet again."

Agent 08189 was immediately up on three of his tentacles and shouting, "Ooo me, me, me! Let me go there. I want to do more on the thing called 'fried breakfasts'!"

The Senior Agent had heard enough and a tentacle reached forward and the recording equipment stopped.

"I think that we should conclude that if this planet's major language is awash with pedants arguing over grammar, there can hardly be much great thought communicated. I think that it is time to reluctantly move on to Venus."

"No, to move reluctantly."

"Oh, shut up."

REPORT ENDS> OFFICIAL STATUS> APPROVED> INVASION DELAYED (INDEFINITELY)

*   *   *   *   *

In his Independence Day Speech, the President of the United States of America, William J. Hewitt addressed recent reports that NASA had been tracking activity on the planet Mars. Widely dismissed as another conspiracy or hoax, the President was in bullish mood addressing the issue.

"Let me say this to you now. Maybe there are creatures living on another planet. Maybe they have seen what we have here, I am sure that they would be jealous of all that we have achieved on this planet. I can tell you this though, I know the reason that they have never set foot on this planet – they have never dared! They would have taken one look at the great military that we have in this country and they would know that you never mess with the USA. That is what is keeping them on their planet!"

The crowd cheers.

The Making of Cheese Market of the Future

"Hi, my name is Anastasia Swindon and I'm reporting for the RWG Network on the making of 'Cheese Market of the Future and other stories', the book that has taken the literary world by storm.

Join me over the next half hour as we get exclusive behind-the-scenes access to the making of the book, interviews with the characters and gain insights into what made this such a literary tornado."

*   *   *   *   *

"Here we are in the Cheese Market in Abergavenny where the title story of the collection is set. It's a big, cavernous hall and my first impression – just from a random Pensylvannia girl – is the smell. My golly this place smells of cheese! There are cheese stalls all around, so I suppose that it must be no surprise but ... here ... I am going to talk to Linda, one of the main characters in the story. Linda! Could you give us a word for the RWG Network?"

"I ... sure, what would you like to know?"

"You're here in the cheese market itself, I believe that in the story you never actually come here."

"That's right ... err ... sorry, your name badge is backwards ... thanks Anastasia, yes, I don't ever come here, but I have taken a break just to pop over and look at it."

"It smells a bit, wouldn't you say?"

"Yes. Here's a secret for you – don't tell anyone – but it's not all real cheese?"

"Not real cheese. Well, stay reading folks, this could be an exclusive for us!"

"I'd say it's pretty obvious – can you imagine the cost of having all this cheese shipped in? No, some of it is stunt cheese."

"Stunt cheese?"

"Flown in specially from Yorkshire. Bite into it and you will get a mouth full of plastic. It's used to bulk out the descriptions. There is loads of cheese here – hence the smell – but be careful with that gouda."

"Careful with that gouda – it could be a book title!"

"No."

"So thank you Linda, there you go readers, a genuine exposé of stunt cheese being used in the market descriptions. We are going to move on through the market now and talk to one of the stallholders. He only has a small part in the story, but I will see if I can get a word with him now. Excuse me, excuse me ..."

"Hello, love."

"So, you appear as one of the stallholders in the story. How have you found the experience of being in fiction?"

"Don't know what you mean, love. I'm just here, selling my cheese. That's really the end of it."

"Did you know that there was stunt cheese being used here? Don't you feel that this is a bit of a fraud on your customers?"

"I've no problem with it, honest. You can't expect all the cheese to be real, some of it is going to be faked and, you know, there are other scenes where people's imaginations fill in things."

"Wow! There's a revelation! You are getting it all today on RWG. Thanks, Sir. Don't go anywhere, this is turning into some read."

*   *   *   *   *

"I'm sitting now with Dudley Didcott, who has done much of the organisation behind the cheese festival here. Dudley, we have heard some pretty revealing things here today, but can you give us an idea of how all this came to be?"

"Thanks Anastasia. Well, it is a simple enough story and it comes down to someone named Dewi Heald."

"She's known as 'the author', I believe."

"Indeed. Dewi was having a conversation with the mysterious 'Dr C' about ten to twelve years ago and they were talking about science-fiction stories. Dewi said, 'there isn't enough comedy science-fiction' and Dr C replied that there was plenty. I think that we can agree that Dr C was right about that. Dewi said that there was not enough **Welsh** comedy science-fiction and this was really where the cheese market came from."

"That is fascinating."

"Yes, quite."

"Anything else?"

"Not really."

"Oh."

"I have a limited range of responsibilities in the text, really."

"Okay."

"Mmm."

"Yes well, there we go folks, an exclusive live report from RWG has brought you a thrilling insight into this year's hot-to-go literary sensation. I've been Anastasia Swindon and I've enjoyed your company, I hope that you have enjoyed mine. Goodbye for now or as they say in Abergavenny ... ta ra chuck!"

Hidden Bonus Track

[This book is the second of a series of three classic books that have been hailed as the greatest works of literature since Chaucer [citation needed]. The first was entitled 'Janet Chittock Likes Your Status' and sold so well that it is now near impossible to find a copy on sale, either in physical copies or online. As no-one will part with their copy willingly, you may have to start looking in charity shops in about twenty years' time for a copy.

This story is part of the conclusion to 'Janet Chittock Likes Your Status', in which the author brings together themes around isolation, homelessness, progressive politics, cookery and peace studies. It is a literary *tour de force* with few rivals. Named after the famed yoga guru and presenter of Radio 4's acclaimed astrology series 'Janet's Planets', the book is rightly now seen as an out-of-print classic loved by everyone who has read it ... except Janet Chittock [lawsuit pending]].

Young Schrödinger

Erwin Schrödinger felt the cold westerly wind against his face as he made his way to see his friend Max for a beer. Max would tell him, of course, that it was Jena's microclimate that was to blame, that somehow the siting of the place in a river basin meant that the wind would ... he forgot how it went, it was Max's speciality, not his.

Sure enough, Max was waiting with two big glasses filled. Erwin had arranged the meeting with some anxiety and so Max knew to have the beers lined up when his friend arrived.

"Hi, Max."

"Hello, Erwin. Think you could do with this."

"Thanks, it has been a tough week. I need this ..."

"You know what I say, you read too much Schopenhauer, that man makes you too gloomy."

"It's about Anny."

The two friends sat down on a spare set of seats and placed their beers decisively on the table between them.

"Yes, well Schopenhauer is hardly respectful of them, is he?" responded Max.

"I know, but ... anyway, I didn't want to talk theories."

"I thought that you were all set for marrying Anny in April."

"Yes, I am, I should be. Well, I think that I should be."

Erwin pushed his glasses up his nose and took a long swig of the beer. His friend stared at him carefully.

"You're not talking about going to Stuttgart again, are you?"

"I am, Max. I am doing okay here but it is time to rise further. The war is done, we have peace, it should be the time to study."

"And Anny objects?"

Erwin placed his beer to one side and leaned forwards. Moments of significance like this needed a certain gravity and precision. He clasped his hands together and pointed the fingers at Max.

"Max, you do not know this but Anny finished with me last year."

"What? Why ever would she do that?"

"I ... Max, this is ... embarrassing. You know ... you know that I have been somewhat ... unconventional at times."

Max now moved his own beer glass out of the way and looked over at his friend intently. Yes, he had worked out in a short time that Erwin was not the most conventional of men, but he had put it down to his brilliance as an academic. He raised his eyebrows as if to say both 'go on' and 'you can trust me'. Erwin talked quietly and awkwardly.

"I ... asked her ... asked her ... if ... err ... someone else could join us."

"Erwin! You fool! What were you thinking?"

"I just, I just found myself sometimes wanting someone else," replied the young scientist, barely making eye contact with his friend.

"Women like to be treated with reverence, you know that. A bit of respect too. No wonder!"

Schrödinger took a long, deep breath and then reached over for his beer. This time he took a long sip on it. Max shook his head sadly before asking the question that would naturally follow his judgement.

"So has she said 'yes' now?"

"I don't know. That's the thing, really. I don't know. She finished with me, then we got back together. We were doing all the usual things that romantic relationships have in them and then ... then she says that she does not want to move to Stuttgart and I wonder if we are in a relationship and ... I have no idea."

"Does she still want to marry you?"

"I'm not sure. She might ... she might not."

"My goodness Erwin, you are talking crazily. How can you be like this? You're a scientist man, pull yourself together!"

"I'm lost, Max. I just don't know whether I am in a relationship with Anny or not."

"Erwin, you are a brilliant scientist but a crazy man. You cannot apply the rules of physics to romance."

"What should I do? How can I be certain?"

Max drank the rest of his beer and looked around to summon the attention of someone to serve them some more. He would be sorry if Erwin did move to Stuttgart, he had enjoyed their chats.

Sometimes he thought that the emptiness of his own personal life was because Erwin had enough adventures for the both of them. Perhaps the man simply did not like loneliness. He had a solution.

Max banged his glass down heavily on the table.

"You know what, Schrödinger, you crazy, lonely fool," he said, with new certainty, "have you ever thought about just getting a cat?"

AFTERWORD

This book has been made possible by the thoughts, actions, statements and sock choices of many hundreds of people. If I tried to thank everyone involved then it would fill another book.

So thank you ...

Why not buy another copy of this book for some of your favourite people? It makes an ideal present for a distant relative at Christmas and a poor substitute for an Easter egg at Easter.

If you have nice things to say then please send an e-mail to dewiheald@gmail.com

You can also follow me on Twitter @DewiHeald1

If you did not enjoy this collection of random thoughts and writings, then you should contact our complaints service by writing to -

David Cameron

10, Downing Street

London

SW1A 0AA

If you liked this book, why not buy a copy for someone you love?

If you disliked this book, why not buy a copy for someone you hate?

Printed in Great Britain
by Amazon

68441750R00118